"Sharon Drew has written an inspirational and well-written book this sophisticated guide. It was an instant success for me. If yo made, how change happens, and how buyers buy—you must re:

    —**Alen Majer,** author of *Trigger Events* and *Selling is better than ...*

"*Dirty Little Secrets* should be a best-seller: The content and delivery is quite good, and so many people and organizations need to hear this!"

    —**Tery Tenant,** Attainment, Inc.

"This book is an insightful, dead-on analysis of how buying decisions get made. The systems approach makes people re-think the entire buy-sell dynamic. The examples are wonderful and I love the direct and personal style. The whole thing screams experience, wisdom, class, success, and authenticity. Best-seller?"

    —**Anne Miller,** author of *Metaphorically Selling*

"Wow, talk about getting outside the box! Sharon Drew Morgen has turned traditional sales thinking upside down and has provided a realistic tactical roadmap for sellers to help buyers get the internal buy-in they need for a buying decision."

    —**Michael Norton,** CEO and Founder of CanDoGo.com

"If you thought you knew all the leading sales methodologies, think again. Sharon Drew Morgen turns conventional selling on its head by teaching us that it's about helping your buyers manage their internal issues before they can buy anything. *Dirty Little Secrets* is a must read."

    —**Rich Dougherty,** CEO of Expert Choice

"This book is fantastic! Sharon Drew teaches support for a buyer's decision-making. Great stuff!"

    —**Kathi Kruse,** Kruse Control Inc.

"*Dirty Little Secrets* takes us inside our buyer's decision-making process where we discover the factors they need to address prior to making a decision—most of them having nothing to do with our product or service. You'll discover numerous strategies to help prospects deal with these issues leading to faster decisions, minimal competition and more sales!"

    —**Jill Konrath,** author of *Selling to Big Companies*

"For the first time, Morgen finally reveals all the *Dirty Little Secrets* of the buying process. As a veteran seller for 20 years, this book gave me a complete new look on selling and buying. Excellent work and highly recommended!"

    —**Geert Conard,** CEO of Geert Conard Management Solutions

"Morgen's ground breaking book teaches how to understand how decisions are made in an organization and how to manage change, with insights and strategies you won't find elsewhere. I've been using this new model in my business and already see almost unbelievable results. Instead of selling, we are actually teaching our customers how to buy."
—**Peter Casebow**, CEO of GoodPractice

"*Dirty Little Secrets* provides insight into issues that are often ignored or misunderstood in the sales process. It will challenge the assumptions and rules we've learned from all sales methods. If you want to understand how decisions are really made and willing to complement your sales skills, this is a must read."
—**Mary Anrigo**, Director of LastMile Xchange

"Sharon Drew continues to provide the cutting edge thinking in sales. Her points are not only valid, but practical. I never realized how buyers really think and make decisions—I do now! The extra benefit of this brilliant book is I can use this with my staff, wife and kids!"
—**Reg Athwal**, Chairman of RAW Group and OneTVO

"Revealing the secret to how people really buy has been untouched... until now! *Dirty Little Secrets* delivers powerful insights and practical thinking that transform not only selling but all forms of decision making. Those who read this book will reap the professional and personal rewards!"
—**Lee J. Colan**, author of *Sticking to It: The Art of Adherence*

"As a Partner in a global executive search firm, I have been struggling to understand how decisions get made in an environment of 'NO.' *Dirty Little Secrets* has not only led to my understanding, but has led to closing several engagements that have been floating around for almost a year."
—**Deborah Sawyer**, Managing Partner of Ogders Berndston

"She's done it again. Having pioneered the new sales paradigm more than two decades ago, Sharon Drew is back with a very human, accessible and powerful approach that helps sellers and buyers collaborate. We've all been in the dark too long. It's time these secrets were revealed."
—**Britton Manasco**, Principal of Manasco Marketing Partners

"As a management consultant, I know how challenging it is to uncover, let alone explain, the behind-the-scenes issues buyers face internally. SDM has nailed it. By reading this book you will come away with a far better understanding of the change management issues a buyer must contend with before they can ever consider buying. I found the book exceptionally engaging, tremendously insightful with a very unique perspective, and well worth reading."
—**Jim Altfeld**, CEO of Altfeld, Inc.

"Morgen leads the field in giving us insights into what really goes on inside the prospect's decision making. This is not a business-as-usual book. She is asking sales folks to make a dramatic change, moving selling away from its dismal yet commonly accepted closing rates. Someday we will all use Buying Facilitation® as part of our sales tools. Get this book and learn how now."
—**Reg Nordman**, Founder and Managing Partner of Rocket Builders

"This book is disturbing. It pulls back the veil: we'll never be able to go back to the old way of just selling a solution. This book teaches us what has been missing from the industry for so long— how buyers decide. The ideas in this book are too big to push under the rug: it's sophisticated, but necessary for any serious sales professional."
—**Jeff Blackwell**, Founder of SalesPractice.com

"*Dirty Little Secrets* is a must read for any CEO or senior executive. Sharon Drew exposes the reasons why sales methodologies fail and provides deep insight into buying, decision making, systems and the change management every customer must go through before making a purchasing decision. The ground breaking concepts in this book are supported by real world case studies that provide buyers and sellers new innovative ways of addressing internal change management issues."
—**Mark Dallmeir**, CEO of The ROBB Group Holdings, LLC

"Sharon Drew's Buying Facilitation® model is not only insightful, it works: it's the only approach that manages the off-line buying decision process. We've been using her process for 10 years and the approach has helped us consistently grow revenues WITH our clients. *Dirty Little Secrets* is the latest in Sharon Drew's long line of best-of-breed business writings and should be on the desk of every CEO and sales professional. After twenty years of writing and speaking about managing buying decisions, Morgen is THE thought leader behind our new thinking of helping buyers buy."
—**Jack Hubbard**, Chief Experience Officer of St. Meyer & Hubbard.

"*Dirty Little Secrets* is an interesting, innovative, thought-provoking, and sophisticated book on systems, change management, and leadership. Although it is nominally a sales book, Sharon Drew maps out the route for how change happens in a way that supports the integrity of the whole system. It's ground-breaking work, and a must read for anyone who is a true student of change."
—**Alan Allard**, President of Genius Dynamics, Inc.

"Get powerful insights and practical steps to helping buyers have an easy time buying—and have a good time while making money. This great book will alter everything you know about selling!"
—**Chip R. Bell**, author of *Take Their Breath Away*

" Social entrepreneurs and progressives often get uncomfortable about sales techniques and wary of 'manipulating' people. *Dirty Little Secrets* teaches how to serve customers by facilitating their decision-making, with no persuasion or manipulation—how to do good, make money and keep integrity intact."
—**Gil Friend**, CEO of Natural Logic

[OTHER BOOKS]

BY SHARON DREW MORGEN

- *Sales on the Line: Meeting the Demands of the '90s Through Phone Partnering*

- *Somebody Makes a Difference*

- ***New York Times* Business Bestseller**
  Selling with Integrity: Reinventing Sales Through Collaboration, Respect, and Serving

- *The New Sales Paradigm Series:*
  - *Changing the Thinking*
  - *Changing the Process*
  - *Changing the Skills*

- *Buying Facilitation®: The New Way to Sell That Influences and Expands Decisions*

CONTRIBUTER TO

- *Chicken Soup for the Soul at Work,*
  by Jack Canfield, Mark Victor Hansen, Maida Rogerson, and Martin Rutte

- *Chicken Soup for the Mother's Soul,*
  by Jack Canfield, Mark Victor Hansen, Jennifer Read Hawthorne, and Marci Shimoff

- *The One Piece of Advice You Need to Earn Your Clients' Loyalty,*
  edited by RainToday.com

DIRTY LITTLE SECRETS

WHY SELLERS CAN'T SELL AND
BUYERS CAN'T BUY, AND
WHAT YOU CAN DO ABOUT IT

[SHARON DREW MORGEN]

MORGEN PUBLISHING
Austin, Texas

Morgen Publishing, Austin TX
Copyright © 2009 by Sharon Drew Morgen

Cover and interior design: Michael Warrell, Design Solutions—Chicago, Illinois.
Cover photo: Courtesy of Siri Stafford, GettyImages.com
Illustrations: Shawn Dibble.

ISBN 0-9643553-9-6

Printed in the United States of America.

Printing number
10 9 8 7 6 5 4 3 2 1

[CONTENTS]

| SECTION THREE |

THE SKILLS: PUTTING IT ALL TOGETHER

PREFACE

IT'S NOT OFTEN I find a sales book that really gets me excited. But that's exactly what happened when I read *Dirty Little Secrets*.

First, a bit of background: I've had extraordinary success as a salesperson. I know what works, what doesn't and how to make things happen. As a leader in the sales field, I've spoken at numerous annual sales meetings and trained thousands of salespeople. My own book, *Selling to Big Companies*, is a Fortune-recommended bestseller.

Yet Sharon Drew Morgen is one of those rare people who really makes me think—and even question the premise on which our entire sales methodology is based.

In *Dirty Little Secrets*, her groundbreaking work, she takes us inside our buyer's decision-making process to a level we've never been before. We discover all sorts of factors that have to be addressed prior to making any changes. And most of these issues have absolutely nothing to do with our product or service offering.

When our prospects disappear into a black hole, that's what they're dealing with. And, as Sharon Drew points out over and over, our sales cycle is as long as it takes our prospects to figure these things out. Often these challenges are so daunting, that they decide it's easier to stay with the status quo—even if it's not a smart decision.

Up until now, we haven't had strategies that taught us how to deal with these "systems" issues that our customers face. We know how to get them interested in our offering. We know how to uncover their needs. We know how to showcase our solutions. But we don't know how to help them get "unstuck."

In *Dirty Little Secrets*, Sharon Drew actually teaches us how to help our prospects have the important conversations that shorten their decision-making process, eliminate turf wars and get buy-in to the change initiative. And, she shows you how to get all the right people on the buying decision team—after just one call.

It's good stuff! This new approach is radical though. It takes a while to get your sales brain around it because it's different from what you're used to.

By adding these strategies to the front end of the sales model, I can see how we'd be able to close at least 2x the business. Sharon Drew's clients get between 200%—800% increase over conventional sales. I didn't think that was possible—and it's not, with the sales model.

This book is not a conventional sales book. If you're looking for a quick fix or want to just take away three things to do better, this book isn't for you.

Instead, *Dirty Little Secrets* actually teaches you how decisions get made, how change happens, and how buyers choose a solution. It alters your thinking about your job and gives you a new set of skills to use with your customers.

Read this book. Savor it. Keep it near you. Use it with your sales skills and have all of the success you deserve.

Jill Konrath
Author, *Selling to Big Companies*
Founder, SellingtoBigCompanies.com

READER'S WARNING

I OFTEN HEAR sellers say that they think buyers are stupid.

You've said that also?

Did you ever think that sellers are also stupid?

I bet not. I bet you thought that we were the smart ones.

But we're both dumb. And it's not our fault.

We know how to sell and how to understand a buyer's needs. Sadly, through experience, we've realized that doing all that, knowing all that, and being really smart and kind and professional doesn't necessarily close a sale.

Oh—it does sometimes, like when we make those quick, easy sales that just fall into our laps. But when that happens, we're just getting lucky.

The rest of the time we're just hoping. Or a victim of circumstance. You know all that.

But buyers aren't really stupid. Nor are they incapable of making decisions. They just aren't making the decisions we want them to make, in the way we want them made. Instead, they are making decisions according to different criteria than we'd like.

Buyers are struggling also; no one has taught them how to recognize and manage the off-line, behind-the-scenes change issues they must address as they deliberate a new solution. And because sales handles merely a sliver of the tasks that a buyer must accomplish, we haven't had the skills to help.

So we sit, helpless, while we wait for our prospects to return with their decision.

As a result, despite all our hard work, we fail somewhere around 90% of the time. But it doesn't have to be that way.

THE SALES MODEL IS INCOMPLETE

I'm going to show you how to have different, much more successful outcomes, make more money, and have more fun. And serve your clients better.

I'm going to introduce you to the missing pieces in sales—the dirty little secrets that have kept us locked-in to the type of results we've gotten used to. I'm going to teach you how teach your buyers to buy.

But be warned: this is not a sales book. This book will teach you different material than you've learned in sales, and you'll need to wear a different hat as you read.

WARNING

Dirty Little Secrets will teach you how to understand and influence the mysterious systems buyers live in so they can efficiently manage the internal stuff they must make sense of—their old initiatives and the new economy, management and colleagues, and partners and old vendors—on their way to a purchasing decision.

It will give you insight into the rules behind decisions and the steps to a sale. It will give you the knowledge to construct a dialogue to lead your prospects through their change. It will give you a new skill set that will help your buyers buy and give you the success you deserve.

In *Dirty Little Secrets* I will introduce you to the many secrets that keep us far less successful than we should be—the assumptions, rules, and activities that are endemic in the sales model that cause you to fail.

I began writing this book with just one secret in mind, one secret that we all know but don't acknowledge: *sales only manages the solution placement end of the buying decision and ignores the majority of the confusing, risky, and hidden change issues buyers need to address behind-the-scenes before they can responsibly bring in a new solution.*

But during the writing process, I realized that the fallout from that secret created many other secrets—secrets biasing buying decisions, relationships, and change. Together, these 'secrets' drive the book: I will unwrap each of the problems that the sales model itself creates, and give you a new tool kit to address them.

Unfortunately, because this is not a sales model, the skills and information will be unusual for you and may stretch you a bit. Fortunately, this skill set has been tested over 20 years and proven successful by many of the largest corporations in the world. But be warned: you will try to fit your familiar sales skills into resolving these problems. I warn you to resist.

- Do not, do not, try to put this material into your 'sales skills' thinking.

- Do not use it to understand a buyer's need.

- Do not try to figure out how to use this to place your product.

- Do not think you use this material already. The moment you ask questions to seek to understand, you are doing sales and attempting to manage the solution placement.

THIS IS NOT A SALES BOOK

I hope you read this book to learn new skills to help your buyers navigate their off-line decision making. Don't confuse this with a sales book. This is a sophisticated guide through managing the change issues and decisions that determine a buying decision—or any decision for that matter.

This book may challenge you, so let me offer you some choices. Section One gives you a complete understanding of what is going on in the buyer's culture as s/he goes through the decision making and change management end of the choice process. If you don't like that level of detail, you may prefer to begin in Section Two where I discuss the system of sales, or in Section Three where I have a full Case Study.

Do what works for you. I want you to use the book in a way that will help you serve your buyers better and be more successful. Dip in, move out, play around. If I had my choices, you'd start at the beginning so you'd have the full set of skills to help your buyers. But do what works.

Welcome to the hidden world of how decisions get made, how change happens, and ultimately, how buyers buy. Let's unwrap all of the dirty little secrets that sales builds in to how we sell and how buyers buy that keep us all less than successful. Let's learn how to add some new skills and start fresh, and have the success we all deserve. Enjoy.

INTRODUCTION

YOUR SALES SKILLS are good. You know how to understand your buyer's needs. You know how to get in front of decision makers, and get past gatekeepers. You know how to pitch and present and handle objections.

But your closing rate is abysmal, and you waste too much time on prospects that won't close.

Take heart: It's not you. It's the sales model. It's the assumptions and the rules, the timing and the focus—the dirty little secrets—that cause you to fail. It's the fact that sales manages only the solution end of a buying decision and ignores the internal, off-line issues buyers need to address before they are ready to buy.

We haven't known we lacked the full range of tools necessary to help buyers manage their buying decisions. We've lost untold amounts of business as a result. We didn't know that buyers don't know how to buy for the same reasons sellers don't know how to sell.

But the profession accepts our common failures and makes us think our results are acceptable, part of the job, and not our fault. Since everyone else in the field is ineffectual in the same way, it seems normal to have overlong sales cycles, objections, and hot prospects that disappear.

Corporations have built 90%+ failure rates into their sales projections, happy when they can get a 15% close rate.

There is no other profession that covers up for a 90% failure rate. Imagine if doctors, or lawyers, or dentists, or even baseball players, had an acceptable norm of 10% success.

THE READER'S JOURNEY THROUGH CHANGE

There is no other profession that covers up for a 90% failure rate. Imagine if doctors, or lawyers, or dentists, or even baseball players, had an acceptable norm of 10% success.

I assume you'd prefer to be closing more sales than you're closing now or you wouldn't be reading this book.

That means you have a problem. A need, if you will. And this book may offer you a solution.

I have a solution. I've got a decision facilitation model that will help you close far, far more sales than you've ever closed. It will:

■ uncover more needs than your prospects thought they had,

■ differentiate you from competitors because you can listen, ask the right questions, and recognize the hidden dynamics your prospect must manage,

■ decrease the close time by at least half,

■ prevent all objections,

■ get the members of the buying decision team to your first meeting,

■ be 200-800% more effective than any sales model on the market, and

■ make you a true relationship manager and servant leader to your buyer.

My solution can do all that. And I can give you testimonials, references, client sites and names, and the features, functions, and benefits of the model.

But my solution is not a sales tool—although it will help you sell.

My solution is a change management model that helps buyers maneuver through their offline issues to get the requisite buy-in to make a purchase.

This book will tell you what they are going through and how to help them do it so you can serve them better and close a lot more business. With your support, buyers will make far more efficient decisions and avoid potential disruption on their way to purchasing a new solution. Win-Win.

To learn all this, you're going to have to 'buy' a new solution from me.

How do you know it's worth the risk to change?

WHAT IS GREATER SUCCESS WORTH?

Before you are willing to buy in to my 'solution' and be willing to change, you'll need answers to these questions:

Are you really willing to change what you've been doing for so long? If it goes against your current beliefs of what 'sales' is? If changing would be difficult and confusing and uncomfortable? Really?

Will your boss have a problem when s/he sees you doing something that differs from what you were trained to do?

What if your boss won't give you a chance to prove yourself with new skills? Or your teammates don't want to change the group-selling approach and don't want you doing anything different?

What do you risk by doing something new? Is it worth it?

Until you have answers to these questions, you can't face the risk of doing something different, whether you have a need or not.

Until or unless all the pieces of your system (your personal habits and beliefs, your work environment and boss, your pride and your ego) buy in to adding the new ideas and skills, and are prepared to go through an uncomfortable process of change, you will not change. Regardless of your need or my solution.

Knowing the details of my solution will not help you manage your personal systems issues. Even if I know the details of your need, I can't help you manage your personal systems issues.

It's not because my product and your need aren't a fit.

Even if I understand the details of your circumstances, and I understand your frustration, and I gather data about what's stopping you from being as successful as you deserve, I won't be there when your boss has a serious discussion with you, or your sales team takes over the sales call from you, or you get frustrated when learning the new material.

I can have the best sales solution in the world—I do I do!—and you can have the exact need that will fit with my solution—you do!—but if your internal system won't buy in to you changing, you will be at risk if you use it, and you won't buy: The perfect match between my solution and your need will be moot. And all of the pitching, presenting, teaching I can do about my model will be a waste.

If you decide that my material will give you the results you seek, you will need to change. Change, even to make you more successful, means disruption.

DOING SOMETHING DIFFERENT MEANS CHANGE

Indeed, until you seek, understand, and agree to whatever changes you would need to make as you approach internal change, you won't know how to apply the information about the new solution I can offer you. Until you do, you won't buy my solution.

Unfortunately, the sales model doesn't give either of us the ability to help you decide if doing something different is worth the risk of change.

No matter how frustrated you are with your current results, no matter how great and appropriate my solution, your status quo will fight to keep things as they are.

Do you want to wait until after you've learned my material to get buy-in from your boss or your colleagues or your ego? How big a part does this internal 'stuff' play in influencing your choice of a solution? Or if you want to change at all?

In *Dirty Little Secrets* I will challenge the unconscious decisions that dictate your current behaviors and drive your results. I will challenge your attachment to the sales model. I will certainly challenge your understanding of the success that's possible. I will teach you about systems, not sales; decision facilitation, not solution placement; helping buyers discern their own answers, not yours.

As you read the book, you may be confronted, confused, challenged and annoyed and want to return to what you're familiar with, even though your current situation caused the 'need' to begin with. It's comfortable. It's predictable. It's you.

I'll hold your hand. I'll give you great customer service. I'll give you a great product. I'll understand your need. But you're the one who must change.

Are you willing to change to be more successful? To make more money? To serve your clients better? Is it worth the risk? Do you know all of these answers right now?

As you manage your learning challenges, you'll get a deep understanding of how change happens, and either be ready to buy my solution or not. And as you're learning and deciding, note *you are going through the same process you require of your prospects each time they consider purchasing your solution.*

You will feel many of the same resistances and confusions that buyers face as I present my ideas and ask you to 'buy' them: how your 'need' resists change; how you keep gravitating to what's comfortable and fight doing anything different; why bringing in a new skill and upsetting your normal routines would be your last choice.

WHAT THIS BOOK IS ABOUT

During the course of the book, *Dirty Little Secrets* will introduce you to the reasons—the secrets, if you will—why both buyers and sellers fail to find the easiest route to problem resolution and possible solution purchase.

In the Conclusion, I will give you a list of these secrets. But given how endemic they are within the fabric of the book, they will not be explicitly highlighted. By the end of the book, they will have all been resolved for you so you can help buyers:

- ascertain their decision criteria to elicit buy-in and manage change as they consider purchasing a solution,

- weight and recognize their internal people and policy obstacles,

- assess the level of risk for each internal element (jobs, relationships, initiatives, people) that touches the new solution,

- make win-win decisions throughout the stakeholder teams,

- manage problem elements early to assure buy-in,

- quickly ascertain the right people who must buy-in and be on the buying decision team,

- recognize and control all of the elements that touch a need to ensure there is no disruption to the system,

- get the appropriate buy-in up, down, and across the management chain.

Dirty Little Secrets uncovers the heretofore hidden parts of how change decisions get made that have nothing to do with needs or solutions, and everything to do with navigating through the off-line, hidden, private issues buyers (or anyone) must address before bringing something new into their comfortable environment.

It's that behind-the-scenes place where buyers go to get internal agreement—while we wait. They need to do this anyway; we might as well learn tools to have some influence over this part of the buying decision process. Indeed, you will learn to help buyers determine how, why, when, and if to buy.

Is it sales? Well, no. It's change management. It's decision facilitation. It's systems alignment and congruency. And you will have the ability to lead buyers through their decisions by adding this skill set to the front end of your sales skills.

In *Section One*, The Buyer's World, I'll introduce you to how a 'need' gets created and established in the buyer's culture, and what needs to happen to be ready to resolve the 'need.'

This section is about systems, decisions, need, and how change happens. By understanding the elements in the buyer's system (the people and policies, rules and initiatives, vendor issues and partner issues), we can help them navigate through their off-line issues to make the decisions necessary for a purchase.

It will introduce you to many hidden change issues having nothing to do with their need or your solution that buyers must handle before they can resolve their problem. We've not been involved in this area before.

Section Two, The Seller's World, is what sellers need to know or do in today's selling environment. It includes a preview of the Buying Facilitation® Method (the change management model I developed to help lead buyers through their buy-in decisions) to give you an idea of what's possible; a look at the 'system' of sales and how it keeps our failed behaviors in place; and a walk through the issues we face as we adopt Sales 2.0 strategies.

Section Three is a Case Study of a buying scenario, including every type of relationship, decision, and outcome from the buyer side and the vendor side. I've included two chapters that show Buying Facilitation® in action to clearly exemplify what you've been learning in the book.

TAKE NOTE

First: Throughout the book I tell a lot of stories about how I lost sales while using conventional sales methods. If you read these stories carefully, they explain the systems issues I failed to help the buyer address; this will give you insight as to how to do it better. I wish I knew then what I know now. Use my mistakes to learn from.

You will hear some crazy stories in here—a major insurance provider cancelled a Buying Facilitation® program because the pilot gave them a 600% increase in sales and it blew apart their system; a president of one of the largest banks in the world failed to implement an initiative for two years at the cost of $1billion because he didn't want to handle a three-year-old union problem.

I promise that each of the stories is true—and cost me many millions of dollars in lost revenues. You'll see from my mistakes how fundamental the (buying) system is, how it is at the very heart of every decision.

While I do offer one recent Buying Facilitation® success story in Chapter 9, the majority of the stories in the book show my failures. I could have included many, many stories of my successes and those of my clients: I've been using this model and teaching it since 1985. But by showing you exactly what happened in each failure, you will be able to see where and how your sales fail and possibly glean some gems that you can use in your next sales situation.

Next: The final Case Study will put everything in the book together for you, and show you what success looks like. For more success stories and additional tools, visit my daily blog: www.sharondrewmorgen.com.

One more thing: This is a book about facilitating decisions. I've put it into sales, but remember you can use this for negotiating, coaching, OD, or just helping your three-year-old decide to clean her room. *At the end of the day, no matter how much our buyers have a need and we have the best solution, if they don't know how to decide to make a new choice, it doesn't matter what we've got.* And sadly, as you'll see, their decision to choose us is rarely about our solution.

It's time to help our buyers make the up-front decisions they need to make before they are ready, willing, or able to buy from us.

Are you're still reading? Good. We have a lot of work to do. Let's get started.

THE BUYER'S WORLD

"Customers don't follow orders, and there's no limit to the ways, media, contexts and reasons why and how they can make decisions that lead to purchase (or, conversely, to abandonment). Information sharing doesn't end with the work day and isn't limited to the channels chosen by your marketing department. And the content that factors into those decisions are often, if not mostly, outside of the purview of marketing and instead originate in other departments (sourcing, vendor relationships, prices, service and support, employee-relations issues, environmental practices)."

—Jonathan Salem Baskin

CHAPTER ONE

MY STORY: HOW I LEARNED TO HELP BUYERS BUY

[WHAT WE KNOW]

- If sellers are professional with a good product/service, they'll be successful.

- If sellers understand a buyer's need they can pitch product appropriately so the buyer will understand the fit.

- Sellers don't close as many sales as they should be closing.

[WHAT WE HAVEN'T KNOWN]

- Buying decisions are not necessarily based on need.

- There are things in the buyer's culture that neither buyer nor seller know what to do about.

- Sales doesn't help manage the offline buying decision issues.

- Buyers live in a complex system that monitors all activities.

- Until buyers are able to change without disruption, they will not buy.

[WHY IT MATTERS]

- ▦ Buyer's environments are more complex than ever, and they have no easy route to change.

- ▦ Buyers could use our help maneuvering through their internal issues because they have a confusing time figuring it out on their own.

- ▦ The tangle that keeps the buyer's problem in place holds more business for us once buyers know how to untangle their mess.

I LEARNED THE HARD WAY how complicated buying decisions are and why the sales model fails as often as it does: sales does not manage the off-line decisions buyers must make.

Sales focuses on product/service sale. Unfortunately for us, that's the last thing buyers need. Literally.

When I started out as a sales person, I thought I knew the job: have a good product or service, be a values-based professional, understand the need, get chosen over the competition. But it never brought me the results I thought I deserved given the amount of time I'd put in. And I sure lost a lot of business that I should have closed.

I didn't know what I didn't know. I understood my offering and the buyer's explicit need; but like all other sales people, I sat and waited as buyers managed the subjective, hidden dynamics on their own, and hoped that they called back.

I hadn't realized that the eventual buying decision really had nothing much to do with me or my solution. It certainly was more complex, and certainly more unconscious, than either the seller or the buyer understands from the viewpoint of resolving a 'need'.

Where did buyers go when they had an urgent need, liked me, and liked my solution—but never called back? Although I made lots of guesses (they sought a cheaper solution, they went to a competitor, they did nothing) it was a mystery until I became an entrepreneur.

As an entrepreneur, I realized what I didn't understand as a seller. I realized that a product or service purchase is based on initially unknowable 'stuff' that takes place off-line in organizations. Indeed, choosing a solution is a change management issue for the buyer.

When I became an entrepreneur, I learned exactly what happens before buyers can choose a solution, and why, as a seller, I inadvertently faced more failure than I deserved. Here's what I learned.

MY STORY—FROM SELLER TO BUYER

I was fired from every job I ever had until I got into sales. And then it was as if I'd found my home. I became a million dollar producer within two years. I was truly on top of my game: money, membership in a prestigious squash club (necessary in the '70s in New York City), designer clothes and shoes. I was a happy camper.

But there was always something in the back of my mind that I found a bit odd: I couldn't figure out why perfectly smart people became dumb as buyers, or where they went when they said "I'll call you back."

It made no sense: I understood their situation and it was obvious to me that my solution could solve their problem. I had good relationships with prospects, followed them up as per agreement, and responded to their requests. I even let them beat me at squash!

Wasn't it obvious that they should be buying—especially the ones I was so close with? And yet why some of them called back to buy, and others—sometimes ones I was closest with—disappeared forever, remained a mystery. Where did they go?

Several years into my sales career I was offered the chance to start up a tech recruitment company in London, Stuttgart, and Hamburg. I was a new entrepreneur, and was fortunate to find great people—one of whom was the brilliant man I was married to at the time—and an interesting business model. We were very successful. And my new role opened my eyes to the problems I'd experienced as a sales person.

My environment was hectic. My American investors showed up whenever they wanted to; my husband and I started going through a bad patch; I was hiring technical people but had no technical expertise; I had no idea how to manage people from other cultures; I was responsible for growing a business and answering to others and making payroll, and and and. Like all entrepreneurs, I was over-whelmed, all the time.

MY NEEDS WERE A SMALL PART OF SOMETHING BIGGER

Yet my company had needs: a team-building course, a marketing vendor, part-time tech people, decorators. Each need, each problem, seemed to have some sort of relationship with everything else in a sort of tangle. I wanted to do team building, but should I include my possibly-almost-ex husband? He was part of the team, after all. Maybe I should wait until we decided if we were going to get a divorce, or just assume we would keep working together—which we did really well—no matter what happened.

And the entryway desperately needed new tables and lamps, but we were going to be moving and weren't sure what sort of furniture we'd need for the new place. Still, we really needed to get some couches now, but weren't certain how big we were going to grow, or how many people would be housed in the main office versus working off site. And because we were growing the business and adding new services, we weren't ready to hire a marketing team, but we needed to start positioning ourselves…. You get the point.

I called vendors to come meet with me so I could more clearly understand my options. [Note: this was the '80s and we didn't have the internet.] They came in to help me begin to make some sense of my choice criteria. They were focused on selling their products.

From the seller's perspective, my needs were simple: a team-building course, new furniture. They gathered data and asked great questions about my 'need', my criteria for purchase, my price points, the users, and what my outcomes were. The folks were lovely. They gave great pitches and offered professional information and marketing material. They followed up, sent stuff, took me to lunch. They were fun, professional, and great Relationship Managers.

THE MISSING PIECE IN SALES

Even while these vendors were pitching, I kept thinking about how to resolve the internal issues that created my needs, and wondered what sort of new problems a solution would create. It certainly was not as simple as just buying a solution. In fact, buying a solution would cost me more than not buying one in some situations.

Interesting for me, I didn't know how to figure it all out: The trickle-down ramifications of any decisions were overwhelming.

When I originally called the vendors, I was gathering data to understand my options about how much I should budget, what changes I'd need to make, who I liked. I certainly was not ready to buy when I met them.

Sad to say, I ended up acting like my prospects acted with me when I was a sales person. I became a 'stupid buyer' who seemingly didn't know how to decide. I kept hearing myself say, "I'll call you back" and putting the decision off until... until either things worked themselves out somehow or the choices would be obvious.

> The sellers didn't help. They treated my need as if it were an isolated event that could be resolved by understanding it and then offering the best solution.

Ultimately I had to figure out how to manage whatever change would result from bringing in the new solutions, to fix problems without creating more problems or upsetting what was already working well. And I had to get buy-in from the appropriate folks, some of whom I didn't initially realize I needed to include until I was far along in the decision cycle.

In my small company of 50 people, just like in every buying environment and in every human system, everything was related to, and touched by, everything else.

If I made a change in one part of the system, there were consequences that trickled down and sometimes blindsided me. Every decision, every element of change, had to fit with everything else. Moreover, each problem that I addressed affected the next one, so I was constantly surprised and needed to re-evaluate every previous decision.

Before I could buy anything, before I could choose a vendor, before I could resolve my needs, I'd have to handle all of the change issues—with people and policies and relationships and moving— that were swimming in the same soup as my 'need.'

The sellers didn't help. They treated my need as if it were an isolated event that could be resolved by understanding it and then offering the best solution.

If they had been able to help me figure out how to resolve my crazy internal issues that were twisted around my Identified Problem (the tangle of needs and pain and deficiencies), I could have made a buying decision more quickly.

WHAT SALES NEVER TAUGHT ME

Sales never taught me that a buyer lives in a system—a unique company culture (or family culture) filled with politics and rules and relationships and hopes and dreams and history—that needs to buy in to change before anything gets fixed or added.

Sales never taught me that buyers had 'stuff' to handle behind the scenes before they could buy, stuff I could never be a part of because I wasn't privy to the buyer's daily work space or relationships. I certainly was never taught skills that would help my prospect handle that stuff so they could buy.

I always thought that if I understood their problem, and talked to the right decision makers, and I helped them understand what was possible with my solution—how they could save money, or be more efficient—that they would know how to buy.

As a seller, I never realized that:

- Choosing a solution, solving a problem, or managing a need is a small part of a buying decision.

- Buyers cannot take any action until they figure out how to manage whatever problems in their system—the tangle of people and policies and relationships that influences and determines the status quo—created the need, and make certain that change wouldn't hopelessly disrupt the work environment.

- Buyer's cultures are so idiosyncratic and unique, and the relationships so delicate and dependent on history, that an outsider can never understand the tangle of issues and elements that make up the status quo.

- Choosing a solution is the buyer's final task, only plausible once everything else is in place.

- Making a purchase is really a change management issue.

- At the start, buyers cannot plan how the hidden dynamics will play out when they contemplate a buying decision.

Neither buyer nor seller has been taught that before buyers are in a position to buy, before a viable solution can be chosen, before budget or vendors can be discussed, buyers must go through some sort of change management.

By focusing on the solution placement—the final activity of a buyer's decision—and not having skills to help buyers maneuver through their off-line change issues which often have nothing to do with the 'need,' we've wasted a lot of time and lost a lot of revenue.

We can help them maneuver through this process, but not by using the sales model.

HOW SALES MUST CHANGE

TWO

[**WHAT WE KNOW**]

- Buyers buy when they have a need that they can't resolve on their own.

- Buyers spend a period of time finding the right solution and the right vendor to manage their need.

- Buyers have a set of givens that define their Identified Problem.

- Sellers sell by understanding a buyer's needs, offering relationships based on values and trust, and resolving the need with their solution.

- Sellers sell by having a trustworthy product/service, brand, and ethic.

- People and corporations are getting risk-averse.

- The economic, political, environmental issues we face are global.

[**WHAT WE HAVEN'T KNOWN**]

- A buyer's 'need' sits in an unknowable tangle of confusing elements and complications that are part of their daily working environment and can't be disrupted easily.

- Until a buyer figures out how to manage this tangle in an appropriate way, they will do nothing.

11

▣ Buyers don't initially know all of the decision factors they will need to handle on route to a purchasing decision; many of them are historic, unconscious, or hidden within departments or groups and don't seem to have anything to do with their 'need'.

▣ Sales tools—product pitch, needs analysis, and information gathering—only handle a small area of intelligence directly around the Identified Problem and become relevant once the buyer gets buy-in from the system.

▣ Buyers decide using criteria based on unique systems issues.

▣ When buyers know how to make decisions that will limit any damage that change will bring, get buy-in from all relevant stakeholders, and be assured to resolve problems better than their current risk-averse work-arounds, they will buy.

WHY IT MATTERS

▣ By not knowing how to help buyers recognize, influence, and manage all of the unconscious, hidden, internal, off-line issues that are unwittingly tangled up around their Identified Problem, we are helping delay the sale, and risk having the buyers make inadequate decisions that don't include our solution.

▣ When facing global financial anxiety, buyers have new and unknown decision criteria and stakeholders. If we can't help them make sense of these issues, we are totally out of control in the sales process.

▣ It is possible to learn new skills to help buyers recognize their internal, unconscious stuff so that stakeholders can buy-in and decisions can be made that will not be disruptive.

THE FOUNDATION of sales assumes that buyers will buy from a seller who understands their needs, is a good relationship manager, and has the best solution at the best price. They've got the need, we've got the best solution.

But if that were true, they'd have bought a lot more, a lot more often, and a lot quicker. But they didn't.

Indeed, sales hasn't taught us that the buyer's Identified Problem—the tangle of issues that hold our buyer's 'need' or 'pain' in place—is only one piece of a broader set of elements within their culture that interact and affect each other, not in an official or even conscious way, but rather like a house of cards: each element influences the rest, and one piece cannot be singled out without the house falling down.

It ends up being a bit like doing a jigsaw puzzle: hard to figure out what pieces are missing until the moment they are needed, when the previously undisclosed picture is suddenly visible and found lacking.

So the Identified Problem is merely one of the pieces that must be addressed on a buyer's route to having a better functioning workspace. But sales has no skill set to manage the full range of issues.

A BUYER'S COMPLEX ENVIRONMENT

Sellers aren't the only ones who aren't aware of the range of issues that go into a decision to make a purchase.

Buyers don't know what they are doing at the beginning of the journey either: They end up feeling their way around in the dark, needing to get somewhere but not being able to see the path. Until they bump into it.

There are so many hidden pieces involved that aren't obvious, even to those that live in the environment, and don't show up until, well, until they show up. Colleagues fight; new initiatives get handed down that delay a long-planned project; a senior person shows up with a new vendor and a mandate; the tech group wants to do it themselves.

Buyers start off thinking they just need to solve a problem, but don't realize the journey they must end up taking to get the necessary buy-in.

Indeed, there has been no model for buyers to use to manage the surprises that seem to explode as people and personalities and policies collide on their way to a solution.

Unless buyers understand and manage the web and tangle of subjective, unconscious, hidden issues that hold their Identified Problem in place, and make sure they will not face chaos when they bring in a solution, they will do nothing.

WE'RE ALL STUPID WHEN IT COMES TO MAKING DECISIONS

Here's a rule that I'm going to repeat several times throughout the book: The time it takes buyers to figure all this out is the length of the sales cycle.

We've worked so hard at understanding need, at finding decision makers and making great presentations.

But still we sit, waiting, frustrated that the buyer is dragging their heels and making stupid decisions while we're really both ambling about trying to take the blinders off and getting adjusted to the dark.

> The time it takes buyers to figure all this out is the length of the sales cycle.

We would have been happy to help it if we'd known how.

Now we'll have a new set of tools. We'll be able to help our buyers understand and manage the broader context of internal influences that affect their ability to buy from us.

We'll be able to help them navigate through their array of decisions and bring together those subjective, unique influences they'd eventually need to manage on their way to a buying decision. Not about the purchase. Not about our product. But about their decision issues, their buy-in, their change management based on the way their relationships and business initiatives are set up. The behind-the-scenes stuff we've never been privy to.

HOW TO LOSE A MULTIMILLION DOLLAR SALE

Here is the sad story of how I lost a lot of money because someone made a bad decision. I had the solution; they had the need. We were good to go. But we weren't.

I was in a very creative prospecting situation recently. The Learning and Development Director of a well-known brewery attended one of my Buying Facilitation® programs with one of his sales managers.

They were very excited, believing the model could be very useful in helping their sellers up-sell and differentiate themselves from their competitors. They also saw the material as an important set of decision facilitation skills for their in-house coaching and consultant groups, their leadership management program, and their negotiating skills. They decided to bring Buying Facilitation® into the corporation as a core skill.

We had a lot of work to do; we needed buy-in from every major team. My prospect (let's call him Dave) and I spent a year planning.

In effect, I did the work of a high level coach as I translated the meanings behind, and designed interventions for, the meetings Dave attended and the people Dave had to influence. I created the Facilitative Questions to help the Buying Decision Team recognize the team, relationship, and change management issues, and Dave did the implementation as an insider.

We kept finding more and more people who needed to be on the Buying Decision Team; the negotiating skills training program had to be factored in to a decision, as did the vendor who had supplied that material we'd be augmenting; the current sales training offerings had to be amended to ensure their message wouldn't be contrary to the material taught; sales managers had to be willing to take money out of their already stretched budgets.

When we got the crucial buy-in from top management, I was thrilled. "Not as happy as I am," Dave said. "This means even more to me—a way to bring my values into this company and have them make more money at the same time. I almost have tears in my eyes I'm so happy."

We continued plotting, planning, whispering, giggling, week after week, month after month. We knew what was going on with each person and meeting.

Yes sir, I was in the loop, in control, on the Buying Decision Team, and in line to not only close a big deal, but to have the opportunity to bring my visionary model into a corporation that would embrace it. I happily spent many hours each week, for months, helping Dave figure out and manage all of the elements of his complex buying decision.

OOPS

All was going well, until Dave decided to take the last leg of the journey on his own, believing that the ultimate decision maker was good to go: Dave assumed that the manager of the pilot group, Jerry, had bought in to the need to add new skills because he had attended some of the early meetings and had had no objections.

But Dave was merely assuming: He hadn't led him through the Buying Facilitation® funnel—that series of decisions necessary before a product gets purchased. A part of the problem was that Dave was relatively unfamiliar with him, given some of the layoffs and mergers that had gone on during the previous year.

When Dave got a note from Jerry telling him to go ahead, that he trusted Dave's capability to do a good job, Dave didn't question what seemed to be an obvious 'buy' signal. But it wasn't. Understanding systems as I do, I waited for the other shoe to drop. I had already guessed that Jerry really didn't know what he was 'buying,' most probably assuming it was conventional 'sales' training.

I convinced Dave to set up a phone conference with me and Jerry, to lead him down the entire Buying Facilitation® funnel so he could make sure my training material would address his criteria and he could buy in comfortably. Then he'd know what he was buying and why.

Dave and I assumed the training was a done deal and moved forward, writing up contracts and discussing training options. But then Jerry canceled two conference calls with me and sent a note to Dave asking for the program price. That was a major red flag: He wanted a price on something he didn't have a value for.

Because I have a rule to never mention price until people have made a buying decision (people need conscious buying criteria to evaluate price) price hadn't been mentioned once during the year Dave and I had been collaborating. Reluctantly, I gave them a price for the pilot program.

You know the rest: Dave was fine with the price. But as soon as Jerry heard the price, he halved the proposed program, and halved the price, stating that with the economy being what it was, there was no way he could risk spending that amount of money. Dave had several meetings with him, but had no Relationship Capital built up because of their new relationship.

Dave negotiated, still not eliciting Jerry's buy-in criteria. Unfortunately, he had to leave on holiday during the negotiations. By the time Dave returned, it was dead in the water.

That was it. End. Finish. Kaput. I got a brief, mournful, email from Dave saying "Sorry". He actually quit the company as a result. And I lost a multimillion dollar deal. It was my own fault: I should have insisted that I meet with the manager to walk him through his decision criteria.

IT'S NOT ABOUT THE NEED

But I never got that chance. Dave had assumed it was a done deal, and omitted the final steps, using his conventional decision criteria and assumptions.

It wasn't about my product, or the client need. We can find lots of blame to go around. But at the end of the day, it was simply the failure of one man to commit. And by that time, I had no ability to influence the outcome.

I had the product. They had the need. They loved me. It wasn't enough. One person didn't buy in. That's all it took. After a year.

As a seller, I was never given the tools to help influence the off-line decisions and relationships that determine how and what buyers choose. I always thought it was about their need, my product, and my personality. I didn't realize that my failure rate had nothing to do with me, and everything to do with whatever was going on that I was not privy to.

But I learned a new set of skills to help buyers maneuver through their internal elements and get buy in. And I'm now going to teach you.

SYSTEMS ARE AT THE
HEART OF CHANGE MANAGEMENT

[WHAT WE KNOW]

- Needs can be resolved when the right solution is chosen.

- Sellers understand how a buyer's need matches the seller's solution.

- To influence a sale, sellers offer good relationship management, a good product, and an appropriate cost benefit ratio.

- Good sellers create values-based relationships and ensure that a buyer's needs match the seller's ability to resolve the problem.

[WHAT WE HAVEN'T KNOWN]

- Identified Problems reside within a tangle of people, policies, rules, assumption, and stories, all of which define a unique system that maintains itself—and the Identified Problem—daily.

- An outsider can never fully comprehend the essence of a buyer's culture.

- The systems that define culture are similar in structure, but the details of each system are idiosyncratic.

[WHY IT MATTERS]

▪ Until or unless all people who touch an Identified Problem are willing to buy in to the disruption that occurs when something new (a solution) enters the system, there will be no buying decision.

▪ Buyers need to understand how to manage their change issues; knowing why to choose a specific solution will not teach them how to manage their buying decision.

▪ Once buyers understand and manage the elements in their system that hold their Identified Problem in place, they can work towards getting buy-in for a purchase.

BEFORE BUYERS even get to the point of choosing a solution, they must get buy-in from everyone in their system that will be affected. Until or unless this happens, they will do nothing, causing the long delays in the sales cycle.

We can help them do it faster if we can help them understand the full range of people and policy issues that are attached to their Identified Problem—and then lead them through their change issues.

I'm going to show you how to help buyers maneuver through their change issues and create buy-in for change. I'm going to teach you how to help buyers accomplish the necessary change management activities so they have all of the people and policies and agreements in place for you to sell them your solution.

All of these things must take place *before* using sales skills. After all, understanding need and making sure the solution is the best one is irrelevant until the system is ready to undergo change. But I'm getting a bit ahead of myself.

SYSTEMS AND THE CHANGE PROCESS

Systems are where we begin. Systems are the glue that determine all decisions and choices and at the very heart of our new skill set. Systems not only create an Identified Problem, but they maintain it through every initiative and every relationship. Let's spend some time understanding their importance.

Once we understand systems we'll recognize the types of issues and job functions and management problems that buyers must address if they are thinking of changing anything. Then we can help them navigate their change issues.

Unfortunately we can't do it for them because we are outsiders (Did you ever try to understand your friend's marriage and make the mistake of giving him or her advice?). But we can be their consultants through the change process.

Think about this from your own point of view when you consider learning Buying Facilitation®. Think about the way the internal 'elements' in your own sales methods—your skills, your work environment, your client relationships, your ego needs—will all be affected when you have a new set of sales skills. It's not about how good Buying Facilitation® is; it's about how you and your internal system can come to terms with the change you'd need to go through.

Through needs analysis and good questions, I can understand your need to close more sales and what the loss of sales has cost you. But I'll never be able to understand your more intimate decisions. I'll never be inside of you or at your meetings with your boss, or privy to your personal reflections. I'll never be able to manage the behind-the-scenes issues with you, or influence your status quo.

By understanding systems, the elements included in systems, and how systems operate, we will understand how a status quo is constructed. We will then be able to help buyers go through the internal buy-in issues they must manage on their way to a purchase.

In later chapters, we will add several other steps to help the buyer maneuver through their decision and change issues en route to bringing in a new solution.

They need to do this anyway. And the time it takes them to come up with their own answers is the length of the sales cycle.

In addition, we'll be adding a front end to sales. We'll be helping buyers manage their change issues first. Then we'll sell. And we'll close a lot more sales, a lot faster, because they will no longer struggle alone with these buy-in issues.

Change Management + Systems Alignment + Solution Choice	Purchase

This new material might seem confusing or mysterious because it is not based on understanding needs or placing product. In fact, we've never been taught this, so it's brand new for you—like picking up a tennis racket for the first time and making sure you don't compare it to when you learned to ski.

With this new skill, we'll have the capability to help buyers manage their behind-the-scenes change management issues. But remember: We can't understand these issues the same way we do an Identified Problem because we don't live there or understand the cultural nuances or have the conversations they need to have. But from our experience in the field, we'll recognize the route they must travel and guide them.

ALL SYSTEMS ARE UNIQUE

Think of a system as if it were a container that holds all past and present elements and choices.

A system is any grouping of people and policies and rules and customs that operate together, define each other, and depend on each other.

It's a collection of stated and assumed elements that make an entity (like a family or a corporation) operate uniquely and behave idiosyncratically.

It's what makes our families different from our neighbors and IBM different from Microsoft.

Many of these elements are unspoken and unconscious. They might be habits, values, historic moments, and unspoken agreements or job titles, vendor relationships, and team competition. Or dress codes and work ethics, relationships and values, assumptions and the history of the founding fathers.

Everyone in a system has implicitly or explicitly bought in to the norms and rules that define that system, and there are no distinctions between functional or dysfunctional elements.

Because the elements are so interdependent, if a problem arises it's difficult for people within a system to figure out what's going on. As a result, change is viewed very cautiously. Shift any element in a system and it causes a ripple effect that leads to unexpected, unpredictable consequences.

I recently started work with a new client. The night before our program he took me to dinner to tell me how nervous he was because he faced impending change. Of course, there was no way to know what we didn't know, and it was impossible to give him empty assurances. But I posed a few Facilitative Questions* to help him discover his own answers:

> *What will you need to believe going in to trust that whatever happens will work out to your advantage?*

> *How will you know that you and your team possess the skills to help you through the disruption that will unfold?*

---

* Facilitative Questions are a unique type of question that I developed to help people recognize all of the internal criteria they'll need to include and address before making a decision. They are unlike conventional questions in that they do not gather information and are not focused on understanding need or placing a solution. Instead they are unbiased, systems based, and used to help people make decisions. I pose the questions in the sequence that decisions follow (see Chapter 6). Each Facilitative Question demands some action. The gleaned data is for the decision maker's edification, not mine. See page 114.

I'm so glad I don't have to be the smart one and have all of the answers. But I can certainly have the questions.

OUTSIDERS ARE NOT INSIDERS

Through typical sales skills, sellers can understand the parts of the buyer's system immediately around the Identified Problem. Of course it's not possible to understand relationships, and history, and nuance that we aren't a part of. It's a mystery to an outsider—like a fish trying to explain water, and a human trying to understand the experience of living in water while looking into the fishbowl.

Think of a system like a bunch of eleven-year-olds in a tree-house with a special language and secret handshake, secret beer stolen from the family fridge, and secret campouts when their parents think they are in bed asleep.

Let's play with the analogy a bit: One of the kids wants his friend to join. The others meet with the new boy and then vote him in. And the vote must have 100% agreement for the system to remain intact once the new kid joins. With the addition of the new kid, the club-house rules will shift a bit to make room for his uniqueness—to a point. If the kid is aligned with the values, behaviors, and underlying beliefs of the others (which presumably he is or he wouldn't have been invited in), he'll still have to do a bit of changing to fit in completely. If he doesn't conform quickly, or in any way threatens the system as a unit, he's out.

SYSTEMS DEFINE NEEDS

The system is sacrosanct. The individual pieces are all replaceable, but together they form a culture that is idiosyncratic—like a brand, if you will.

Cultures are systems that contain, organize, and buy in to the elements that define it.

Take out any one part of the system, and the system gets defined differently: the personality and uniqueness of the system will shift.

Cultures are systems that contain, organize, and buy in to the elements that define it.

When a new child gets added, the family system changes. When a new person joins a department, the dynamics of the system shift to fit the new personality; and the new person will also be forced to adapt to, and mirror, the behaviors, values, and beliefs of the rest of the department.

It's usually a little bit of bending on both parts, but the rule of thumb is that when anything shifts, the system will face some sort of disarray and will fight the new element until the new element bends to the will of the system—or leaves. So the Identified Problem that our buyers want to resolve sits in their system with some degree of comfort.

I was fired from many jobs in publishing because my distinctive personality was generally unable to meld into existing systems of the journalism of the '60s and '70s. But once in sales, my type of personality was the accepted norm. Unique, eccentric, a bit pushy, bossy, a bit arrogant, smart, well dressed, and deeply spiritual. So long as I maintained the values, the persona, the rules, and the work ethic—and brought in the bucks—I was entitled to my unique personality.

HOMEOSTASIS

When we approach a buyer with a solution to a problem, that problem has already been built in to the system and has been there long enough to affect other departments, other initiatives, etc.

As a result, the ramifications of change may not be obvious, initially. Sometimes it takes a long time for them to emerge, and the confusion is part of the length of the sales cycle. Buyers will make no purchasing decisions until they get buy-in from the components (people, policies, initiatives, partners, teams) that are in any way connected to their need.

A system will fight any proposed change until it knows how to manage disruption and maintain balance at least at the end of the change process. Balance is the primary objective of a system.

We learned in high school biology that systems seek homeostasis: The ability of an organism to maintain internal equilibrium by adjusting its physiological processes.

Change brings disruption to some part of the system, leading to the loss of homeostasis. That's why change is so often avoided. Systems will sabotage or reject anything new that enters without buy-in. The cost is too high: Teams stop working together; people sabotage the project. Rather than face that level of disharmony, the buyer keeps using the old hardware or the old training program until they can figure out a route to balance.

Any change, any addition, any solution must be able to maintain the integrity, and balance, of the system. Once a system understands how it can end up in balance, it's more willing to change. Buyers face internal change management issues as they bring in something new (a solution) to ensure a minimum of internal disruption.

Make no mistake: The integrity of the system is much larger than any of its pieces. A manager who challenges the system and continuously creates disruption, even if she is creative and innovative, will be let go.

Indeed, until the costs of failure exceeds the costs of change, the system will attempt to ignore the need to change.

> Until buyers understand, and know how to mitigate, the risks that a new solution will bring to their culture, they will do nothing.

The right solution might show up to resolve the problem, but it might be the wrong solution for the business environment. Or the timing might be wrong. Or too many departments will get disrupted. Or a rollout might be affected. Or an external supplier is fixing what an internal group is scheduled to handle and budgets get affected.

Buyers will buy nothing, even at the financial expense of maintaining the Identified Problem, unless they end up with a fully functioning system when they are done.

Unless the new solution can maintain systems congruence with minimum fallout and maximum buy-in, buyers will not buy: Their need is irrelevant, our solution is certainly irrelevant, and time frame is largely irrelevant. Until buyers understand, and know how to mitigate, the risks that a new solution will bring to their culture, they will do nothing.

It is only when the members of a system determine that change will lead to a higher level of excellence and KNOW HOW TO GET FULL BUY-IN, that they will undertake the change process and consider bringing in a new solution.

ELEMENTS THAT TOUCH A PROBLEM MUST BUY-IN TO A FIX

Why do we need to consider the parts of the system that don't seem directly related to the Identified Problem or to our solution? It's for the same reason that you must worry about your boss or your colleagues if you consider learning Buying Facilitation®.

If I were using sales tactics, I'd seek to understand your needs to close more or faster, and then target my product pitch to your need so you could see the relevance of my solution. Then I would manage the relationship and give you a good price.

But that's not enough to help you decide. There are bigger deciding factors involved.

Unless

1. your boss can see that you will be at least as successful using a new skill set,

2. clients appreciate you helping them at a different level than they are accustomed to,

3. other team members don't mind when you sound different from them,

4. you can still maintain the company brand, and

5. you are willing to internally confront your personal beliefs about your skills, your success, and possibly failures, and be willing to go through an uncomfortable change process,

you will not get agreement to use Buying Facilitation®, regardless of whether or not it's the right solution to meet your need.

If we can help your boss and teammates, your ego and beliefs, recognize how a new set of sales tools would fit into the values, rules, assumptions and goals, the change will be welcomed and the system would remain in balance.

Because of the ripple effect, many elements that are not obviously a part of the Identified Problem will need to be a part of the solution. Without full buy-in, the system will reject the fix because it will be out of balance.

Let me say that again, as this is pivotal: Systems will not allow anything in—even if the system appears to be broken and in need of a solution and the exact right solution shows up—if the underlying system would be severely threatened by the change.

Now we know where our buyers go after saying 'I'll call you back.' They are engaged in preparing their system for change in order to ensure that adding a solution will not cause chaos.

BUYERS DON'T DISAPPEAR

Let me tell you a story of how important systems are.

Early in my training career I made a very expensive systems error. I trained a pilot group of a large insurance provider. They had 1,500 sales people; we piloted 15. Following the program, their sales went from 110 visits and 18 closed sales (the normal 7% success) to 27 visits and 25 closed sales (a 600% increase). This is a success story, right? Wrong.

The company canceled the rest of the training because those sorts of numbers left the system out of balance. First, the sales folks were annoyed because they were hired to be 'field reps' not 'telephone reps.' They WANTED to be in the field for four weeks instead of one week!

Next, they were being paid on number of visits (!), and the accounting people couldn't pay these 15 separately (on closed sales) from the other 1,500. And finally, they were closing so many more sales than everyone else that the system broke down: The other sales reps couldn't compete, and if they all adopted the new program, there wouldn't be a need for 1,500 sellers. Some would have to be let go.

Instead of changing the system to incorporate a 600% increase in sales, less travel time and expense, fewer sales people, and less overhead, they fired the manager who hired me and halted further training. They maintained the integrity of the system—no matter what the cost—because they didn't know how to change in a way that maintained homeostasis. I had created chaos and disruption: They threw me out of the system and went back to their status quo.

Silly, right? But they weren't silly, I was the silly one. That's what systems do. They maintain homeostasis at all costs.

I was so busy solving the 'need' that I didn't manage the systems issues first. I should have spent far more time delving into the systems issues than I did understanding the 'need.' Rather than assume that the sales folk were paid on closed sales, I would have found out that they were paid for visits. (Imagine sales folks being paid for visits!)

Also, I should have asked the decision team to plan for a substantial increase in results if the pilot worked BEFORE starting the program. I should have gotten the sellers' buy-in to change their job description to telephone rep instead of 'outside sales rep' BEFORE the program. I should have had the company's agreement to pay the control group differently from the other 1,500 sales folks BEFORE starting the program. Then the route to change would have been built in with minimal disruption. I ended up sacrificing the larger goal for a tiny pilot and didn't manage the systems issues.

Instead, the system got rid of the manager and me—the irritants to the status quo.

A PERSONAL CHANGE ANALOGY

To help you understand at a gut level how important homeostasis is and why a system will fight change just to maintain its integrity, I've included a simple analogy. Try to put yourself into the story with your own change issues, and learn about your own internal system to get a sense of how pervasive the rules of systems are.

Let's say that you're a couch potato. During a routine medical exam, your doc tells you that if you don't exercise more you're possibly at risk for heart disease. The next day, your spouse surprises you with a membership to the local gym. There you go! All set? Nope! Here's why:

1. If you had wanted to work out, you would done so already (An Identified Problem resides within the system that created it and maintains it.).

2. You may have some unconscious issues around exercise, working out, going to the gym, how you see yourself, etc. You may not even be aware of all of the underlying issues! But all of your beliefs, identity issues, and ego issues hold these unconscious exercise avoidance issues in place. Every day you create work-arounds and rationalizations to maintain your status quo.

3. In order to work out habitually, you will need to shift your beliefs about yourself or exercise or health. You will have to weight your choices against spousal relationship, health and aging, medical advice, and social pressures. You will have to start new rituals, new habits, and create new rules and norms. What seems like a simple act of exercise becomes a multifaceted Identity issue.

4. If you agree to work out because you're told to, prior to shifting the internal dynamics that have maintained your status quo without exercise, you will fail. You will either quit after a couple of weeks, get an injury, start working extra hours so there is no time for gym, and so on. A systems management approach is needed to make exercise habitual, separate from health or medical issues.

Someone outside the 'system' cannot fully understand why you haven't been working out (You don't have time; you don't like the gym; you have an old injury; you're fine the way you are; your Dad never worked out and lived 'til he was 90). And if anyone tries to convince you, you'll object.

Until or unless there is buy-in, and you are ready, willing, and able to change the appropriate elements of your system (in this case, all of the factors that maintain your weight, unhealthy eating, lack of exercise, and self-image as a couch potato), you will not seek or accept a solution to your problem.

Since the Identified Problem is being managed by continuing to be a couch potato or not 'liking' parties or having a great new (size X) wardrobe or working longer hours and getting more done, there is no urgency to do anything. It's not about the gym membership. It's not about the doctor's advice.

What is the Identified Problem here? All of it: the health issues, the clothes, the embarrassment, the self-image, the excuses, the solitude. The system is dysfunctional and maintains the integrity of the whole, regardless of the poor efficacy of the system.

The Identified Problem is a tangle of systems issues that have bought in to 'couch potato.' You would have to reconfigure your entire system to buy in to change if you were to become a person who went to the gym frequently and ate a healthy diet. For this to happen, you would have to:

1. Change your core identity and become a Healthy Person;

2. Recognize what you got out of being overweight, and why you would be willing to make a change now;

3. Accept the time commitment to exercise and new eating behaviors as part of your daily routine and upgrade your internal system of how you plan a day;

4. Find a way to buy-in to the probability that in the beginning you will have discomfort and pain;

5. Get support from your family and friends about the time to exercise, and about designing/eating new foods to help you manage the weight loss; and

6. Develop a good self-image.

As a general rule, before deciding to make a change, members of a system must agree that things need to be better and to know how to avoid permanent disruption by ensuring that the system will return to homeostasis once the change is complete.

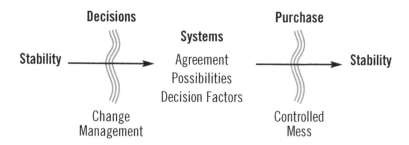

In this analogy, the system would have to shift the beliefs, relationships, and behaviors that keep the overweight person overweight, in order to be willing to change. The person would also have to agree that he is overweight, not healthy, and unhappy about change.

It's important to note that an Identified Problem results from a series of probably unconscious—certainly unwitting—decisions made within a (buyer's) system way before you met them. Decisions created the Identified Problem, and decisions will keep it in place or change it.

Indeed, the Identified Problem is merely one aspect of a broken system, and everything around it holds it in place. For change to be considered, the system must consciously or unconsciously recognize the core values they need to maintain and ensure their survival through the change process.

In other words, when a buyer has a need, it won't get fixed until everything in the system that touches it and is affected by it gets taken care of as part of the problem resolution.

THE ELEMENTS OF SYSTEMS

Why do we need all of this detail about systems? To help buyers buy, we're going to help them manage their buying environment, which is a system.

Remember: The system has created the Identified Problem and has tentacles from many areas that touch it and will fight to keep it in place in order to exist.

If the buyer was able to resolve his problem he would have done so already. If the system allowed change or felt enough pressure to change or search for excellence, it would have done so already.

I'm always curious about why buyers find us *now*. What stopped them from being ready *yesterday*. And why is the system willing to forego its comfort *now?* Buyers so often seek information to give themselves the ability and excuses to *not* buy a solution now.

Here are some of the elements of a system. Let's use this to understand how systems keep such a stranglehold on the culture.

In his excellent book on culture and leadership, *Organizational Culture and Leadership*, Edgar H. Schein says that a culture is:

> "….the accumulated shared learning of a given group, covering the behavioral, emotional, and cognitive elements of the group members' total psychological functioning …a history of shared experience." And so, a system.

Language: Cultures share a common language, a way of speaking and using words that have special, often hidden meanings. Stories often define the status quo. The way people speak with each other, as well as their expectations, conform to the norms of the system. Language is the vehicle people use to interact with each other and to re-enact the culture daily.

Customs, Traditions, Rituals: Sometimes dependent on historic incidents, sometimes newly created, these practices are unique to the culture and difficult for outsiders to understand or recognize. It's the company picnic. It's the way people are promoted. It's the bell that rings when a sale is made. I had a client who gave each newcomer a roughly hewn foot-long, flat, wooden horse. Their job was to decorate the horse—paint it, glue stuff on it—and add it to the other horses on the Winner's Wall. Each time someone made a sale they would go over to a large, hanging bell, clang it loudly, and move their horse forward. Everyone would take a moment to look up and cheer. That instilled friendly competition on the team—a custom that had been going on for years.

Relationships: There are unique bonds between each of the members of a culture but they behave congruently within the rules that define it. Sometimes these bonds are political or hierarchical or job related. Members of a system 'have each other's backs' and will coalesce around the maintenance of the status quo, unless they are in competition. Then they may sabotage an initiative, or hold up a project. Sometimes competing managers hold up a project while they each try to take ownership.

This is an important aspect of a corporate system. Don't overlook it.

Rules, Assumptions, Values: Parents have one set of rules, kids another. Senior managers have one set of rules, employees another. Every culture carries a set of overriding rules, values, and assumptions that govern the dress codes, relationships, and operating procedures. Outsiders and newcomers cannot understand these easily because they are largely unconscious and idiosyncratic. But make no mistake: To be a part of the system, you must conform. Until the '90s, everyone at IBM had to wear gray suits.

Politics: Who's not talking to whom? How do employees interact according to rank? Who is breaking the rules and who isn't? Who is on the outside? Who keeps the secrets and who divulges them? Who does the boss go to when he or she has a problem? Who is the unspoken leader? None of this is visible from the outside, and yet this consideration can make or break a buying decision.

THE CORPORATE SYSTEM

As you can see, there are many elements to a system, and the choices of how people behave and make decisions within a culture are endless, making it quite impossible for an outsider to understand. Each group or family or corporate culture is unique and idiosyncratic. Certainly nuanced. Much of what goes on is hidden and unconscious. And frankly, it looks pretty crazy to those of us on the outside.

Now that we understand what a system is, let's expand the discussion to how systems define corporations. We'll then have an easier time understanding what our buyers need to go through before they buy.

Each corporation has a unique personality, a set of norms and biases, and expressions and definitions of 'how things work' that incorporate the followers and reject those who don't buy in.

Each department and team has its own unique system of elements and feelings and people and rules that work in unison to define the daily operations of the working environment. To make matters more confusing, each person has her own internal 'system' which is unconscious and idiosyncratic.

No wonder managing change from the outside is impossible.

Remember when you began a new job and had to figure out how to fit into the system? How long did it take you to recognize the real group leader or the trouble maker? To learn how to act at meetings or during brainstorming sessions? Or learn how late people usually stayed in the evenings or who came in on weekends or the politics of working hard?

I once consulted with one of the Big Three accounting firms and was shocked at the number of divorces: Their badge of honor was to work at least six 16-hour days, with prized bragging rights given to those who stayed overnight. It was assumed that wife and kids were secondary. And they all boasted about it.

Corporations will have different rules and relationships and initiatives than their competition does. Think of the differences between Apple and Microsoft or Oracle and SAP.

HOW NEEDS RESIDE WITHIN A SYSTEM

All of these unconscious elements work together in a way that creates and maintains any need, including any Identified Problem that shows up within the buyer's system.

Somehow, at some time, for some reason, the rules and people came together to create the Identified Problem that needs to be resolved. There is implicit agreement to keep it in place—until something else comes along that will be better and that will also maintain the status quo in some fashion so the baby doesn't get thrown out with the bathwater.

Indeed, the Identified Problem is as much a part of the system as any of the functional aspects. It has been seen as functional until now, after all.

This means that before a new solution or fix is brought in, it's vital to ensure that all parts of the system that are connected with the Identified Problem will maintain their roles or status and continue to operate efficiently.

So if Fred has been doing the accounting using a small, insufficient program, and the company wants to purchase a very complex program that will take over most of his tasks, something has to be done with Fred. Do you give him a new job? Teach him the new program even though he doesn't want to learn anything new? Fire him? Not buy the program? This is a systems problem, not a technology problem. And until the company knows what to do with Fred, they will not purchase new software.

As sellers, we've not realized how important it is for buyers to manage their systems: Until the buyer gets buy-in from each part of the tangle of elements that touch the Identified Problem, she will take no action.

What makes this most interesting, is that we'll never understand the details because it's so idiosyncratic; what makes it stranger is that the buyer doesn't understand them either. But I'm getting ahead of myself.

WE CANNOT UNDERSTAND THE BUYER'S SYSTEM

I'd like to put up a red CAUTION flag here: As part of our sales system we have made the 'need to understand' into a science. We know how to listen in order to hear exactly where the problems lie and how to discuss solutions in terms of the buyer's problems and our products or services. We've heard it all. We can hear one sentence and know what the problem is. We are infallible diagnosticians.

But diagnosing 'need' and placing a solution must be delayed while we help buyers manage their internal change elements first.

We'll finally have the ability to start at the beginning of the buying-decision process and teach the buyer how to quickly and systematically address their decision issues and possibly help them get ready to choose our solution.

Let's now look at how decisions get made within systems. As we put each piece of the puzzle together, note that they are like nesting bowls: The system determines the decisions that create and maintain the need. The more we understand this, the easier it will be to lead our buyers through the steps.

CHAPTER FOUR

WHAT ARE DECISIONS?

- Buyers must decide whether to choose a solution.

- Buyers choose solutions that will resolve their Identified Problem.

- The more sellers know about the buyer and the buyer's 'need' the better positioned they are to make a sale.

- Change will only take place when a piece of the system shows up as less than adequate, and the surrounding system elements allow the introduction of something new.

- Systems develop semi-permanent work-arounds to manage problems.

- Identified Problems are maintained daily through work-arounds.

[WHY DOES IT MATTER?]

- Understanding all of the elements that surround an Identified Problem is not enough to help a buyer get buy-in to change.

- Buyers will buy only if we help them understand how their Identified Problem was created and maintained, and help them introduce a new solution that will have full buy-in.

- Buyers don't understand at first how their system keeps their Identified Problem in place. The time it takes them to get the requisite buy-in is the length of the sales cycle.

HOW DO BUYERS BUY? What causes a sale to happen—or not?

What does a 'problem resolution' look like from the buyer's viewpoint?

How do buyers choose one vendor over another? Or choose at all?

For too long we've believed that with the right need and the right relationship, we could sell the appropriate product. Now we know that buyers must first make some internal decisions that have nothing to do with us.

BUYING DECISIONS INCLUDE SYSTEMS MANAGEMENT

I lost a multimillion dollar contract because I was unable to influence an important part of a system. My client was a brilliant visionary. He 'got' Buying Facilitation® instantly, and brought me into a large multinational bank to license my material for small business bankers.

After a few very successful pilots with an 800% + increase in sales over the control groups, it was time to begin training trainers.

The Director of Training had not been involved with our work, but our future success depended on his buy-in, so I kept asking my client Facilitative Questions to help him decide to include the Training Director in our conversations. He ignored me.

As we moved closer to implementation and the Training Director was still not involved, I got concerned. I actually flew to my client's site on my own dime to take him to lunch. When he showed up for his lunch meeting, he was surprised to see me sitting there.

> SDM: "I came to discuss Jim. What would you need to reconsider to make Jim a part of our discussions?"
>
> TONY: "Sharon Drew! Don't worry! I'll handle Jim! We don't need him!"
>
> SDM: "Humor me here, Tony. We need to have him buy in to what we are doing, become an active part of our work, and help us with the decisions we are making or he will sabotage the operation."
>
> TONY: "I know him. Don't worry about it. It's all under control."

And the rest, as they say, is history. Jim got involved too late, hated me and the project, and got rid of me at the first opportunity. All this, after the contract was signed. It was a costly mess for everyone.

WHAT ARE BUYING DECISIONS?

What are buying decisions, when do they occur, how are they executed, how do they determine change, and how do systems factor in?

Until we understand how decisions get made, we have no way to influence them. And sometimes it's hard to consider the types of decisions buyers must make that are outside of the conventional sales agenda.

> The main concern of any proposed decision is the way it will affect the system that must change to accommodate it.

The main concern of any proposed decision is the way it will affect the system that must change to accommodate it.

Before buyers will make a decision to purchase a solution, they must know the answers to these questions:

- Will fixing the Identified Problem disrupt the status quo? How much disruption is the system capable of accepting? How will they know this as they begin considering change?

- What people, policies, relationships, rules will be stressed by bringing in something new? How can the buyer recognize the important issues to take into account when at first there is no way to know what will be involved?

- What sort of mess can they expect? What can they do up front to alleviate this?

- How will the system manage the potential disruption? What else needs to change to maintain balance?

- How can the decision makers take much of this into account before they make any decisions? How does the team gather the right members to make the necessary decisions at the right time?

Until all of this is figured out, buyers will do nothing. The risk to the system is too high.

A decision is a choice that includes the means to change in a way that doesn't permanently threaten the underlying system.

Change is okay so long as the system remains stable. If stability isn't assured, nothing will change no matter the size of the problem or the cost to the system. People keep smoking; companies keep using old software.

DECISION MAKING AND CRITERIA

There seem to be an array of new books on the market that discuss how decisions are made.

They all extol behavioral approaches to getting people to do what you want by doing doing doing something a certain way to appeal to the 'new brain' or the 'limbic brain.' Push, in my vocabulary. Better ways to push.

Current research decision making focuses on why decisions are emotional and on how to pitch, place, or present, accordingly. The underlying belief is that buyers will buy given good information, a rational reason to buy, and emotional hooks.

I disagree. I don't believe that decisions are made emotionally. Instead I believe that decisions are triggered by the personal biases, values and underlying beliefs that have created and maintain the status quo, often irrationally.

Decisions are made only after an automatic, often unconscious, values check has been made. How many of us would make an emotional decision to walk into Lamborghini and plunk down $250,000 on the spur of the moment? Why not?

I believe that:

1. People and systems will not operate outside of their values. Just like my insurance client could not adopt the change necessary for the 600% increase, the system will reject what is out of integrity. All decisions are guided by our values-based criteria even it they are unconsciously assessed.

2. The studies done by so many of the neuroscience books look at the behaviors of people after they made internal, unconscious decisions to adopt change.

3. It is possible to help people recognize their internal, even unconscious systems of beliefs, values, and biases, and then show them a route to buy in to change while maintaining integrity.

4. It is possible to help people re-weight their unconscious criteria and change levels of importance to enable them to make values-based decisions.

Every group, team, family, has a set of unconscious and idiosyncratic criteria that guide decision making. These criteria are a mainstay of the person or group's system. They are based on historic decisions, behaviors, experiences, and stories, that make up a culture and they define how we act as individuals, parents, or team members.

To demonstrate how unconscious criteria shape our decisions when we have what looks like a need, I've put together a simple analogy that will illuminate what's going on within our buyer's buying environments. The analogy will show how the underlying system biases a solution choice even it there is a need for change.

THE CHAIR ANALOGY

Assume you and your spouse are in your sixties. You have three married kids, who all live within the same town. Because you wanted to simplify your life, and your kids have large houses and large dining rooms, you sell your house, and move into a much smaller place, with only one extra bedroom, a small kitchen, and a small dining area. You actually give one of your kids your large dining room set because they have three kids and the holiday meals all seem to take place in their dining room.

You and your spouse had several discussions about this, even a fight or three—there was certainly a case to be made for needing a large dining room—but you were adamant that you wanted to reduce your expenses as you retired.

Let's say one of your kids calls to say she and her husband need to stay with you for three months while their house is getting renovated. Your spouse suggests that you pick up two extra chairs on your way home from work, chairs that look like the other four you already have.

You go to the store. The chairs are now $1000 each, and you must buy a set of four. Do you buy them? Of course not. You go home to your spouse and discuss options: will the small dining area manage all four extra chairs? Would you rather get folding chairs, even though they are uncomfortable for those times guests come by? Do you buy the four new chairs and move the credenza out of the dining area so there is room for all? Do you take the two extra new chairs and put them in a different room? Do you just eat in the living room for three months?

You have decisions to make that have nothing—and every-thing—to do with the chairs you saw in the store; but until you make them, you can't buy anything. Not to mention that your spouse is now starting up another fight about the size of the dining room and why the choice of the small house was a mistake.

Here are the systems elements involved:

1. Current eating arrangements fit four people comfortably.

2. Two people regularly use the table and chairs, and other family members or neighbors drop by daily.

3. The current dining area contains a credenza, small table and four chairs.

4. The argument between the couple about purchasing a house without a formal dining room has not been laid to rest.

5. Two adults will be joining the couple for an extended time period.

The family must assess the following options:

1. Should we reconsider the dining room issue and focus first on a long- term solution such as constructing a new dining room off of the kitchen? How long would it take to complete?

2. Should we turn the extra bedroom into the dining room, and vice versa, for three months?

3. Should we just buy folding chairs?

4. Should we borrow chairs from the daughter who has the large dining room?

5. How can we settle our argument?

Before choosing an option, they need to know:

1. What criteria will we use to make a decision?

2 Who should be part of the decision making team?

To the chair salesperson, it's confusing. The buyer has a need, and he has the chairs, so what's the problem?

Any decision this family makes must maintain the integrity of the family. It's not about the chairs.

UNCONSCIOUS DECISION MAKING IS PART OF THE BUYING DECISION

Unfortunately, in the early stages of 'need resolution' buyers don't always have ready answers for the decisions they need to make—or the knowledge of the right questions to ask. Just like you won't know, before your conversation, how your boss would react to your proposal to learn Buying Facilitation®, or the details of a compromise, so buyers can't know in advance what they will need to manage as they move forward. It sure makes decision making confusing.

I was doing some training and consulting for a well-known European consulting company and helping a team of Senior Partners close business. I received a call from the group leader asking me to help with a sale they had already closed. A major European bank that had chosen my client to develop an electronic banking solution.

Two years prior, my clients had won the bid for a $30 million application and were still waiting to begin the implementation. They stayed socially involved with the 'C' level decision-makers monthly and did small applications for them while they waited. And waited.

In the interim, it cost the bank $1 billion (that's Billion) *not* to implement the solution and their competition stole their business.

My clients wondered what was stopping the bank from moving forward. After all, they were the Chosen Ones: the money had been approved, and they knew the users, the managers, the techies, the market, the goal. They had the solution. What could be missing?

The CEO of the bank and I scheduled a phone meeting. He was smart and fun. I used Facilitative Questions on him to help him figure out what was going on, believing he would not wittingly lose $1 billion dollars in business, especially since there were budgeted funds for a new solution.

About 12 minutes into the conversation, as I guided the CEO through the decisions he'd made and the systems issues he had been dealing with, he put several disparate issues together in his mind. He remembered that there was a three-year-old problem with a union representative, left over from the previous CEO, and until that problem was resolved, they couldn't move forward.

Apparently, the problem included some unresolved personal issues between the two CEOs, and the union rep problem was lumped into the feud and left unattended. The new CEO avoided the old CEO and did a lot of unconscious work-arounds, delaying difficult decisions and elevating easy decisions. I must admit that I found our conversation rather shocking.

One of my Facilitative Questions to this man was:

What would need to happen for you to resolve this problem in a way that would support your bank and give you the legal and ethical means to move forward?

We solved the problem by bringing in a consultant to meet with him and the union reps for a day. Within two months, my client was doing the work.

It seemed so simple. And yet this very smart CEO had 'forgotten' the problem and made decisions that kept it in place.

Years later, I told this story in London during a keynote. A participant in the front stood up and said: "It must have been a bad sales person. A good sales person would have discovered the union problem and solved it immediately." From the back of the room came a familiar voice: One of the Senior Partners from that firm had flown in from Brussels to surprise me. I had no idea he was there.

Waving his arm in the air, he shouted: "I was one of the Senior Partners. And I disagree with the guy down in front. We knew the technology, we knew the business problem, we knew all of the "C Level" people, we knew the managers and the users. We knew the banking environment. Trust me: There was NO WAY to get to a three-year-old union problem from where we sat. Even the CEO didn't realize why he made his decisions. There was no path from 'there' to 'here' using conventional sales or consulting skills."

It's certainly odd that the CEO of a major world bank would 'forget' something like a problem with a union rep or ignore a personal problem with an old colleague. We can argue this for hours.

The lesson is: As outsiders, we can't understand the off-line issues within a buyer's system, but we can facilitate their internal discovery so they can make the decisions necessary to move forward.

To begin, let's see how an Identified Problem sits within the system to a clear path down the route to unraveling all the pieces.

CHAPTER

WHAT IS A NEED AND HOW DOES IT AFFECT THE SYSTEM?

[WHAT WE KNOW]

- Sales has focused on the part of a buyer's system that shows up as an Identified Problem.

- There is no part of a buyer's buying decision that operates without taking into account the surrounding systems issues.

- Buyers are not initially aware of all of the elements that must be included in their solution design.

[WHAT WE HAVEN'T KNOWN]

- Systems create their own problems.

- Systems develop work-arounds for Identified Problems that become a permanent part of the system until the system seeks an additional level of excellence.

- Decisions are based on idiosyncratic internal criteria that must be consistent with the unconscious rules of the system.

- Parts of the system that touch the Identified Problem must buy in to any change or homeostasis will be disturbed.

WHY DOES IT MATTER?

- Once we understand systems, decisions, and needs, and how together they create and maintain an Identified Problem, we can help buyers maneuver through the full range of decisions needed to use our solution to resolve their problems.

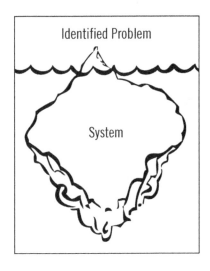

Identified Problem

System

NOW THAT YOU understand the more sophisticated elements of how a need gets created and maintained, here is my comprehensive definition of an Identified Problem: a gap in the functioning of the system that keeps it from functioning at its optimal level of excellence and that uses semi-permanent work-arounds until a permanent fix is chosen. A system will seek a new solution only when current behaviors are judged inadequate.

Think of an Identified Problem as the tip of an ice iceberg: The main body of ice is under the surface and supports the small part we see.

Any Identified Problem shows up as a functioning part of the system, since it is indeed functioning in some capacity. At the point that the system determines that it needs to be functioning better is the point at which buyers are ready to buy. And the systemic elements that have kept the Identified Problem in place will fight for their lives to continue doing what they are doing.

HOW WORK-AROUNDS MAINTAIN NEEDS

I once placed a cold call to a man late one afternoon. The man's secretary responded that he wasn't available. When would it be best to call back? "Any day before 2:00. Just don't ever call after 2:00."

I'd never heard a response like that. Jokingly I said, "What, does he come back from lunch drunk every day?"

"Yes," she replied.

I was dumbfounded. But I managed to say:

"Boy, he must *really* be good at his job in the morning."

"Yes. Very good."

In my map of the world, I'd think that was a problem. But the system—with far different criteria than I would have used—was willing to forfeit several hours a day of this man's work hours. They worked around his problem and designed a system that functioned....the way it functioned.

Long before a problem seeks resolution, the system creates work-arounds to maintain balance. We'll continue to tell ourselves that we'll lose weight when we go on vacation, or that we ARE eating well (and the bread and potato chips are merely an occasional break in routine), and we just need to buy this ONE new outfit in the larger size.

Work-arounds are the system's easiest solution to an Identified Problem. It's those people and policies, ideas and behaviors, which systems put in place to manage the Identified Problem before a more effective solution is sought. It's the system's way of fixing the problem in the easiest way, with the least harm.

Sometimes the system even believes that the work-around IS the solution. Until they realize that it's not. Sometimes we can use Facilitative Questions to help buyers determine they can achieve greater excellence, as we'll see in Section Three.

I'm reprinting a paragraph from the systems chapter here because it bears repeating:

> Once the system determines that a greater degree of excellence is possible, and knows how to attain the buy-in of all the appropriate elements involved, it will start the change process. Indeed, *until the cost of failure exceeds the cost to change, the system will ignore the need to change.*

Buyers develop work-arounds in the meantime. For you, that means you may try different consultative sales tactics to learn how to close better rather than learn Buying Facilitation®. Or your prospect will hire her old vendor rather than going through the process of finding a new one.

The problem with work-arounds is that by virtue of the fact that they are in the system, they influence the system and appear to be a piece of it. They are imbedded in the operating environment and maintain the Identified Problem.

As outsiders, we don't know how long the work-around has been there, the lengths the system has gone to maintain it, or what levels of buy-in it has garnered. Buyers don't always know the tangle involved here either.

Is the work-around simple, involving recent decisions and can easily be undone? Or is it more complex, perhaps the result of a long-standing situation that has several layers of relationship issues and rules wrapped around it that will be challenging to unwrap if a different solution is sought?

In the chair example, the problem began when the couple decided to buy a house without a formal dining room. In the union/bank problem, the Identified Problem began three years earlier when the personal issues between the outgoing and incoming CEOs were not resolved.

As outsiders, we have no way to trace the full history of how the Identified Problem came to be, or how entangled the work-arounds are in the daily functioning of the system. Also, it's possible that the

Identified Problem is so enmeshed in the system that many of the members don't perceive it as problematic. This is often where sales falls apart.

WORK-AROUNDS ARE A PERMANENT PART OF THE SYSTEM

Work-arounds take on a life of their own and are hidden within the Identified Problem almost like a structural flaw.

Like a dog with three legs, or a person with a pacemaker, the system learns to compensate differently to ensure that it maintains integrity one way or the other. It's here that our prospects tell us that they've just begun resolving their Identified Problem by trying a new fix, and need six months to see what the results are going to be.

> By the time we meet our prospects, they already have an environment that maintains the status quo, and the Identified Problem has been more or less resolved.

By the time we meet our prospects, they already have an environment that maintains the status quo, and the Identified Problem has been more or less resolved in some way.

Being excellent or functional has nothing to do with the internal reality of the system: People are happy enough with the situation, or they would have changed it already.

Indeed, as sales folks, we often gather data about the Identified Problem without understanding the importance of flushing out the work-arounds that have been holding it in place. But buyers either can't or don't know how to easily discover these issues on their own and often don't buy what they should or delay their sales cycles unnecessarily. And we are left waiting.

The full extent of these work-arounds, and how imbedded they are, is largely unconscious, as you'll see in this next example.

CLUELESS IN AUSTRALIA

I once coached the CEO of a very robust concrete company in Australia. James wanted help understanding how sales 'should work.' Apparently, in his 20 years as the head of the company, James had never gotten involved with the sales division. He had a manager who took care of it all and called me because he thought something strange might be going on. He wanted my advice.

James became suspicious when the economy was faltering and the sales numbers remained robust even though their customers—construction companies building new houses—had lost half of their business since the year before. He wanted to understand how it would be possible to see positive numbers under these circumstances. Might his sales manager be giving false numbers in order to maintain the group's commissions?

As an engineer, James had thought it best to leave the sales department in the hands of a sales manager and not get involved. Indeed, he'd only had quarterly meetings with the manager in the three years they'd worked together.

It was absolutely fascinating and unprecedented how much he did not know about the sales end of his own company. He really was clueless: How is your competition doing through this downturn? No idea. What is your turnover? No idea. How many sales people do you have? No idea. What is the configuration of inside sales and outside sales? No idea. How long does it take to close a sale? No idea.

I had to work hard at staying objective and lead him through his own process of discovery, understanding that if he wanted different results he'd have to be willing to change his behavior. Frankly, I didn't necessarily believe James wanted to change since he had had ample time to resolve the problem before now.

In our first coaching session, James discussed his fears about getting involved with sales and looking foolish to his staff because of his obvious lack of knowledge. I realized that he had a very limited—and biased—set of beliefs that guided his behavior and had perhaps cost him a great deal of money. As part of his coaching homework, I gave James a list of questions for self-discovery.

To resolve his problem, he'd first have to be willing to admit his lack of knowledge and failures (the systems stuff), let his team know of this (seemed to me most company folks would have realized this already), and be willing to sit down with the sales team to begin the process of unwrapping historic decisions in order to resolve any problems.

Ultimately, James decided to do nothing. He called me prior to his second session, and told me that he didn't want to find out the answers to my questions because if he began prying, the sales manager would feel he didn't trust him. And things were going well enough to not worry about what might be happening.

This is a great example of a work-around. The entire culture was working around his ignorance of sales, and there would be fallout if he got involved now.

I suspect that the answer was more that he didn't want to uncover his own failures, and preferred to maintain internal homeostasis rather than figure out how he himself would need to change to fix any problems. Regardless of the cost, he would continue his work-around of using an unsupervised sales manager to handle issues that went far beyond mere sales support, supervision, and leadership.

> Something we outsiders identify as a problem may not be viewed as a problem from inside.

I couldn't have made this up. To me, it's a scary story. But it proves my point: Something we outsiders identify as a problem may not be viewed as a problem from inside. The preference may be to maintain the status quo rather than face disruption and change, no matter what the cost.

SYSTEMS GO TO ANY LENGTHS TO MAINTAIN THEIR STATUS QUO

We just can't make sense of the idiosyncratic systems buyers live in.

Remember homeostasis? Not only will a system fight to maintain its status quo, but the system will mightily deny a problem: Overweight? It's been a stressful time and when I'm ready I'll lose weight. Pre-diabetic? The doc told me not to worry—I've got years yet before it is a problem. High turnover? The whole field suffers from the same problem. A slow computer system? As soon as we get the new techies they'll be able to fix it, and in the meantime we don't need the programs quickly anyway. A 10% close rate? The industry average is seven percent, so we're doing well. Long sales cycles? Industry standard.

Here are some corporate requirements that might need a solution but have work-arounds imbedded within their system. This is not a complete list, just a few common examples:

- team building issues;

- new software needs;

- web design needs;

- marketing needs;

- any type of training;

- any hiring needs;

- needs currently being managed by an existing group (in-house or outsourced) that require a new product or solution;

- all banking needs;

- anything that requires multiple decision makers to buy-in to change;

- anything that changes the status quo.

Rule of thumb: As long as the prospect is somehow managing without your product, they are working around the solution that your product or service can provide. That means that the elements that are part of, or touch, the Identified Problem must agree to let the new solution replace them. Otherwise they are fine, thank you.

A NEED? WHO HAS A NEED?

A colleague of mine in the sales training business had me speak with a sales manager—a long-standing prospect of his—to see if she had interest in learning Buying Facilitation®. My colleague had been 'in relationship' with this woman for six months, but nothing was happening even though he believed there was an obvious need. I knew after the first two questions that she would never buy sales training from anyone:

SDM: How are you currently training your sales people?

PROSPECT: We have never had any training. We have monthly discussions about prospects and products. That's it.

SDM: What has stopped you from seeking additional skills for your folks?

PROSPECT: Nothing. I want them to have good skills. But my boss thinks we're doing so well that he doesn't want to change the way we're doing anything. I thought that I could convince you to convince him to give me some budget, to change his mind. I've tried for six months. Could you try?

Is there a prospect here? Did the client 'need' sales training? According to him, no. He was fine, and had a whole system that he created to maintain his practices.

Think about this for a moment: Is it likely that by using the typical sales model we'd be able to 'convince' him that he wasn't fine? That he would be more successful *and* meet his ego needs by purchasing some sales training?

When I asked my colleague if he'd realized this wasn't a buyer he said:

I don't know she's not a buyer. We are in a relationship. And her company has a lot of money. I can tell she needs sales training. When they finally do have a need, I want to be there.

I asked him how he thought there was a sale possible if the senior manager didn't want to change.

What would need to happen for the senior manager to change his beliefs and actually notice something was missing? Not anything that a seller could manage using selling skills. And my colleague certainly tried—throughout six months of visits and presentations, and pitches.

This is a perfect example of a biased seller in search of a need to resolve so he could make a sale. The standard sales model assumes that a prospect exists:

- because we can see a way for a buyer to be more effective with our solution,

- if we can find a way (through the strength of reason, or our product data, or convincing numbers that prove our product's efficacy) to get prospects to understand we can help them improve.

But this highlights our desire to sell, on our belief that we are right because we can see a better way for the prospect that they can't yet see.

As we now understand, the fact that we see a 'need' that our product can resolve doesn't mean the system is ready, willing, or able to be resolve it.

We know this. It's happened to us hundreds of times. How many times have we kept calling on an assumed 'appropriate' prospect that will never close, hoping to be there when they are ready?

But I can offer you hope. When working with a prospect that doesn't see a need that we can see, it's entirely possible to open up possibilities by facilitating other choices.

In the example above, this manager's system maintains his sales method, yet his ego was focused on 'success.' It's possible to redirect the conversation for him to 'increase success,' and adding skills to what he's already successfully doing. Attempting to push your solution just makes his internal system defend itself. He has to recognize his internal beliefs, understand his work-arounds, and learn what other elements touch his Identified Problem. He must learn how to make a new decision that will keep his system intact.

A BUYER'S NEED SITS IN HER SYSTEM

Sellers

When we *sellers* operate within the sales model, we cast a biased eye toward what appears to be a need and use learned techniques to develop discussion, interest, communication, trust and relationship—all in service to use placing our solution: We assume that we can sell to a buyer with the right need.

We then focus our attention on needs that might benefit from our solution. Sure, we often hit the target. And very often we are accurate: The buyer has an issue or a need, and something from outside could make it better.

As we see now, this process takes place in a vacuum: The sales model treats the Identified Problem as if it were an isolated event and the rest of the buyer's system didn't exist. The system is always much bigger than the apparent 'need.'

All of the objection handling, relationship building, pitching, and information gathering can't manage the underlying hidden system that holds the Identified Problem in place.

Buyers

Buyers needs are based on a different set of biases, albeit sometimes unconscious and outside of the buyer's normal understanding. But make no mistake. The rules of their system and culture will be the bedrock that any change decisions get made on. These issues have to do with people fighting over turf, old vendors that are beloved, tech teams that want to do more than they have time for.

It's not about having a problem we can fix. It's about having a system that wants to keep doing what it's always done.

HOW SYSTEMS CHANGE

1. *A need isn't elevated to the rank of 'needs fixing' until there are several indications from within the system that the system is operating poorly.*

I remember once judging a woman because she was smoking. I couldn't understand why such a lovely-looking woman was smoking (Do you hear bias in here?? My Mom had a heart attack from smoking.). Then I found out that she had been in a car accident in which her husband died, and she had been hospitalized for six months near death. And when she got out of the hospital, she learned that her teenage son had run away after getting on drugs.

She had no criteria around stopping smoking at that point in time. Even if I 'understood' the woman's problem, I would have no way to offer her solutions because she had to manage a very personal (internal systems) issue that had nothing to do with cigarettes.

2. *A solution must fix a need in the easiest, most effective way and create the least disruption to the system, regardless of what it looks like from the outside.*

Another funny story seems far less funny as I approach old age. As a very young woman, I was walking across the street with my handsome boyfriend, and watched as an old woman in short shorts walk toward me. "Yeeew," I said loudly, "Look at her! The nerve of her to be wearing shorts like that at *her age*." As she passed me, she said, "You wait until you're my age and you're hot." Indeed.

3. *An Identified Problem must be resolved with the lowest cost—a combination of money, time, people, initiatives— and the highest value to the system. And it's never about the money.*

When I moved to Austin, I kept my place in Taos, thinking I'd go back frequently. It never happened. I finally put the house on the market but it took three years to get a buyer. When I got the offer I was given only two weeks to move out. I had no other house to move into, nowhere to put my houseful of furniture, and no idea how to manage a move across states in such a short time.

Luckily, I found a great farm house 25 minutes from my Austin loft, but was told by the mortgage lenders, the banks, the authorities in Taos (don't ask), and others that it would take at least two weeks to get the everything done. Not to mention the packing, moving out, and moving into a new house.

After finding the new house, talking to banks, and such, I had 10 days. I went into action. I got a list of everything that had to be done, and called the 15 people on the list. They each told me they needed one or two days to do their share of the work. Yes, I said, but what if we had the best possible set of circumstances?

What would need to happen for you to be able to do your part of the transfer in hours rather than days?

I put everyone on a Yahoo group, and introduced them to each other, asking them to help me and each other be very efficient. I trusted that each would do their best. I hired a young man that I knew in Austin and we flew to Taos, and packed and went to the dump and and and. And then packed the truck, and drove 15 hours back to Austin, to be met by another group of friends and helpers to unpack.

We didn't sleep for days. And it cost me a lot of money. But in two weeks, one house was sold and the other house moved into (and painted!). I never stopped to think about the finances. There was a larger cost if it didn't happen.

MORAL AUTHORITY IS NOT A GOOD EXCUSE

4. *A solution may involve addressing several internal fixes as well as external fixes, even if the resolution seems like it would be a simple fix.*

I'd like to share a story here about a doctor friend of mine and his problems helping his alcoholic patients stop drinking. Think of this as the doc selling his patient sobriety.

My friend Bill started an alcoholic unit in a state psychiatric facility. Through Bill's vision, the hospital created a one-of-a-kind unit for alcoholics with multiple psychiatric problems. He got funding, staff, and students. His unit was state of the art. I asked him how successful he was.

BILL: Well.... about as successful as anyone else working with alcoholics. They won't change.

SDM: So you see it as the alcoholic's responsibility in the doctor/patient relationship. Where does the doc fit in here?

BILL: I'm doing my job. They have to do theirs.

SDM: And how do you know that the job you're doing is being done in the right way for your patients?

BILL: What do you mean? I'm a doctor. I've been doing this for years. I know what to do.

SDM: So you can see the problem, and you know the solution, and you have moral authority.

BILL: Of course.

SDM: But I hear it's not working.

BILL: Right. But that's not because I'm doing anything wrong. They need to change. I can't do that for them.

SDM: So you're telling them what they need to do through the eyes of your experience and your job description.

BILL: Of course.

SDM: But it's not working. You can be as right as you want to be, and have all of the moral authority you deserve, but if it's not working you need to be doing something differently.

BILL: What do you suggest?

SDM: We can begin with my belief that information doesn't teach someone how to make a new decision.

BILL: Are you saying that me telling them the right thing to do—like to go to AA meetings and to stay away from the situations that got them drinking to begin with—is wrong? That they won't change even though the information is accurate?

SDM: They know the information, and they aren't changing. They need to be able to buy in to seeing themselves as a different person, and have their new beliefs guide their behavior change. Trying to change behaviors while they sit comfortably within the person's internal belief system and daily patterns will be unsuccessful.

BILL: It works some of the time.

SDM: Yes—when the person already has had a belief change.

BILL: So in order for me to get these folks to change, I have to find a way to get them to change their beliefs and let the belief changes promote behavior change. That goes against everything I've been taught, all of my schooling, and what I teach my students.

I can go on with this story for pages. Bill was 'right'. He understood the problem, had the correct solution, had moral authority because he was a professional in his field and understood the problem, and the field bought into his 'rightness.' And yet he failed over 90% of the time for the same reasons sellers fail: His skills did not address the underlying systems elements that created and maintained the status quo, and he had no way in to achieve buy-in.

Who was the one with the need? The problem? It was Bill. He had a whole system that maintained his status quo, with a life-time of work-arounds to support him and continue his ineffective practices. While the solution may seem simple—just teach him how to facilitate the patient's decisions—he'd have to make huge internal changes before being ready to seek a solution.

This story is a parallel to the sales issues we've been discussing. Are you ready to consider shifting the skills and behaviors that have become part of your identity to get better results and add value to your customers? What happens when I suggest you need to change?

Systems don't want to change. Indeed, buyers will go to herculean lengths to keep the solution internal or familiar so they won't have to manage the disruption that a wild-card entering the system would create. It's only when the system is thoroughly convinced it can't resolve the problem itself that an external solution gets considered. I'll be speaking about the reasons why in the next chapter.

DIFFERENT AGENDAS

There is one more problem that makes managing and resolving a buyer's need more complex: Within a buyer's system, like any human system, there are subsystems working simultaneously, and sometimes at odds with each other. An example would be a sales group that needs to spend money on new leads or training, while the corporate execs might freeze the budget.

> One of the big problems with closing sales is that our buyers may have a genuine need, but the decision makers, the system, and the unconscious elements within the system, all have different agendas.

One of the big problems with closing sales is that our buyers may have a genuine need, but the decision makers, the system, and the unconscious elements within the system, all have different agendas.

Today I had a conversation with a Business Development Manager from one of the largest credit card providers in the world. She wanted to take one of my training programs, and had the money in her budget, but the company had frozen all spending. All spending, no matter what the expenditure or the budgeted money.

A perfect example of 'different agendas.' And trust me, this company could have afforded to send the woman to the training. They just didn't know how to make a decision.

It's not about the chairs. And we forget that our product is only one piece of the solution.

Do we have to wait for buyers to find their answers? Yes and no. Buying Facilitation® leads them through the route to manage their problems from within, even when the system doesn't think it has a problem.

We can't do it for them, but we can do it with them and help them do it on their own, and effectively and efficiently, from inside.

CHAPTER

THE WAY BUYING DECISIONS GET MADE

WHAT WE KNOW

- Buyers buy because our solution resolves their need.

- Some prospects call and buy, some prospects disappear.

- By gathering data, building a values-based relationship, and pitching to the need, we've addressed all of the issues involved with a need.

- A purchasing decision is far more complex than we originally realized.

- Buyers are not cognizant of all of the internal issues that need to be managed when they first consider purchasing a solution.

WHAT WE HAVEN'T KNOWN

- Until or unless the tangle of systemic and cultural elements that touch the Identified Problem are managed, no buying decision will happen.

- The system holds the Identified Problem in place and has created conscious or unconscious work-arounds to manage it.

■ The systems behind these work-arounds must be addressed in some way before a purchasing decision happens.

■ No decision to purchase will take place unless the people and policies included in the work-arounds buy in to change and the elements are redistributed in a way the system approves.

[WHY IT MATTERS]

■ The time it takes buyers to come up with their own answers, and figure out how to adopt new solutions without disruption, is the length of the sales cycle.

■ By helping them focus on the Identified Problem rather than first figuring out the systems issues they need to address, we are actually delaying a purchase unnecessarily.

■ Sellers cannot help buyers manage their full range of internal systems issues using conventional sales models.

OBVIOUSLY, we'd rather have someone buy than sell. But because our jobs have basically focused on resolving a problem, we haven't helped buyers manage their off-line buying decisions. Buyers have gone away and done this on their own! And we have sat and waited for them to call back—thus lengthening the sales cycle!

We now know that an Identified Problem resides in a much more complex system than buyers originally understand, and certainly much larger than sellers have been aware of. Unfortunately for us both, buyers don't initially recognize the full range of systems elements they must manage.

When we attempt to gather information early in the buyer/seller relationship, buyers inadvertently end up giving us potentially false, or at best inadequate, information.

Part of the problem is that we've been coming in too soon and asking the right questions at the wrong time. It keeps the buyer focused on a solution well before they have managed their change issues: We may be giving them the right information to solve their problem, eventually, but they just don't know what to do with it at first. They don't know what they don't know.

DECISION MAKING, CHANGE AND CHOICE

Another problem is that buyers are too close to the situation and initially only see small chunks of it with no ability to have perspective and see the whole: When we are looking at just one leaf in a forest, there is no way to know that there is a fire in the next acre.

Unless people are able to move back from their narrow viewpoint and view the entire situation—sort of in a 'witness' or 'coach' or 'observer' position—the status quo may seem fine, thank you.

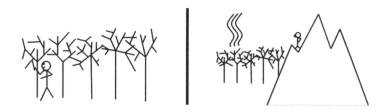

The status quo actually creates a bias and a set of blinders that deflect new possibilities. Sales actually keeps buyers focused on the problem, with no ability to get perspective.

If I tell you the benefits of Buying Facilitation® before you have decided that you are ready to change, or that change is even possible, does my pitch help you buy in to the need to change what you've been doing for so long? Or help you with your boss? Or make you defend your position?

To add something new, or fix something, requires change. To change, the system must be ready and willing to experience disruption. To be ready and willing to experience disruption means the system recognizes a path to excellence and stability. The time it takes buyers to figure this out is the length of the sales cycle. We can sit and wait for them to figure it out, or we can help them.

Our first job is to help the buyer move away from their status quo and get perspective as an objective observer—almost as their own project manager—so they can begin to understand the range of issues they need to manage.

Fortunately, there are specific decision phases that all decisions take as they go through the process of change, regardless of the size of the sale, the cost of the solution, or the complexity of the decision. With our new understanding of systems, we can lead them down their decision phases.

By using the decision sequence as a guidepost to help lead buyers through the path of change, we actually give them the capability of getting the necessary perspective to move away from the 'leaf' to the nearby mountaintop as it were, and see the entire forest through new eyes.

Once they can see the whole picture, they can get the right people involved and the right decisions made to get systems buy-in. So long as we first veer them toward their behind-the-scenes decisions, not toward our solution.

A BUYING DECISION IS DIFFERENT FROM A SOLUTION CHOICE

We waste a lot of time trying to convince buyers to buy, following the wrong prospects, and spending inordinate amounts of time understanding the needs of buyers who will never buy.

Buyers, also, waste a lot of time en route to excellence. As they amble along the change process, they have success in 'fits and starts', with lots of surprises showing up—relationship issues, policy problems, old technology, ego issues. It's not a pretty process, and people and relationships often get damaged along the way.

Remember the story of Dave, the one where I lost that huge sale because the final manager terminated the project? That was a surprise: We hadn't realized he hadn't bought in. It had nothing to do with my solution or their need.

Ideally, buyers would like to make quicker decisions; they'd prefer to resolve their business problem as soon as possible with little fallout. They are not dragging their heels. *They really don't know how to do it quicker.* We haven't had the non-solution-related skills to help them.

When we begin learning about facilitating the buying decision, the hardest part for us is that we're accustomed to trying to 'understand.' We will still do that eventually—when it's time to place our product to match their need.

Sadly, we will not be able to understand many of the *details* of what is going on in the buying system because it's so idiosyncratic. The good news is that we can *facilitate the route through to the buy-in process.*

It's not as confusing as you might think—you already do this in other areas of your life. Think of a time when an upset friend or child told you a story about a personal slight from a friend, or something nasty their spouse did. When you listened, you didn't need the details. You just tried to get them to speak with the teacher, or apologize to the friend, or take the spouse out for a meal.

You knew enough about human interactions and the systems behind relationships to be able to point the way to some sort of resolution, regardless of whether or not you knew the details.

Will you have the 'right' answer to help a buyer through their confusion? No. But you will be able to facilitate the person's route through their own decisions.

For the first phase of the buy-in process, we'll be teaching buyers how to maneuver through their private, idiosyncratic considerations in order to figure out how make the right decisions.

In effect, we will be teaching the buyer how to

1. peruse their culture to discover something missing and see if they are wiling to do something about it,

2. discover the elements that touch the Identified Problem in any way to include them in the decision,

3. figure out the people that need to be included on the Buying Decision Team,

4. understand how the work-arounds or familiar resources are configured so they can resolve problems from within where possible,

5. sift through the appropriate elements needed to get to buy-in for anything coming in from outside,

6. fit our solution into their system where appropriate, and

7. ensure our solution would enhance the system without fallout.

At the same time, we'll help them design an excellent working environment.

THE RULES OF A BUYING DECISION

There are three sequential decision stages a buyer goes through between beginning the process of recognizing an Identified Problem, understanding the specifics of the work-arounds, gathering together the appropriate Buying Decision Team, and making a purchase.

These are *not* the typical steps we're familiar with—recognize a need, provide a fix for it, sell it. Buying Facilitation® manages the full range of issues that created and maintain the Identified Problem and work-arounds.

Buying Facilitation® Decision Phases

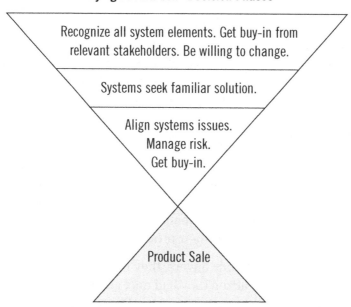

Here are the three stages en route to a buying decision:

- The system (all of the people and policies that touch the Identified Problem) must recognize that something is missing and then believe it's essential, at this time, to add an additional level of skill to the status quo to potentially increase functioning.

- The system must have ascertained that there is no known familiar resource that can fix the problem from within the system.

- The system must recognize all of the elements that hold the status quo in place and that must buy in to any proposed change.

Using these three points, here are the details of what constitutes a buying decision.

Rule 1

Until the prospect can recognize the full range of systems elements that live congruently within their culture and find them lacking, an Identified Problem is not seen as something that is ready to be resolved—regardless of the cost to the culture, or the problems it seems to be causing in the system.

Needs must be recognized and defined by the culture, and be willing to seek change.

This is the most difficult part of the decision equation: If the stakeholders had already decided on going down the path toward change, and had known how to manage their internal issues congruently, they would have fixed their problem already.

By the time we meet our buyers, they have either decided not to fix the problem, not realized they had one, are in the process of trying to figure out how to resolve it (internally, or with other vendors), or don't care.

Be cautious here: The Identified Problem that we notice is only one small aspect—possibly even a tiny part—of the entire problem that has been living and breathing in the system. When we show up with a solution, we really have no clear idea at first what we're trying to resolve. The buyer has also not fully decided that they are ready to change, or they would have done so already.

In order for anyone to consider change, they must first be able to see all of the appropriate elements in the surrounding system and notice if there is a glaring omission. But if it's so ingrained in the system that it shows up as a natural element in the system, nothing looks broken.

If you've always been overweight, it's part of your set of expectations to buy a large size. If you've always had delayed sales cycles, you expect to wait for the buyer to return.

As I've stated before, people usually only see what's directly in front of them, and don't have the capacity to get a holistic view that will show them omissions or problems.

Even knowing there is a problem isn't enough to consider change. They must get buy in from everything that touches it before they are ready, willing, and able to do something about it.

Until they

1. recognize the entire set of issues and understand their interdependencies,

2. notice a gap between where they are and what excellence could be for them,

3. know how to evaluate and manage the rules and relationships that maintain issues,

they will do nothing.

What we don't know, of course, is how a resolved problem would fit into the larger system that has made it possible for the Identified Problem to remain in place for so long. Does the resolution create imbalance?

Let's use you learning Buying Facilitation® to understand the decision phases. Here are a few Facilitative Questions that will show you the type of systems guidance I'm recommending as the first phase:

What is stopping you from closing all of the sales you deserve to close?

How will you know when it's time to add a new set of skills to the ones you currently use when you sell?

What would you need to know or understand from your boss and colleagues to know if they would be comfortable allowing you to use a different sales tool than what they are used to?

How would your boss know before you learned the skill that it would have a good chance of giving you the type of success s/he might require of you?

Note that these questions are all focused on discovering criteria. They help you move away from your biased, insular view, and gain perspective on systems issues you may not have considered—but need to be addressed before any change can happen. And while I cannot know what is going on inside, I can know how to lead you through your own discovery. You're not going to buy my product until you do, so I might as well help you.

WHERE DOES THE NEED SIT IN THE SYSTEM?

We've thoroughly discussed 'need' earlier. Now it's time to ask a different question:

How does a system decide a need must be resolved?

One of the hardest things for our buyers to determine is that their status quo isn't good enough. It is a reminder that they have been less than excellent for a period of time. And everyone has to agree.

This is often one of the most arduous tasks our buyers manage; often they see a 'need' for excellence, but their colleagues or bosses don't. Or they don't want to change.

Even once the right people are on board, they must agree to change and do something different than they are doing now.

Sometimes our buyers don't realize there is a gap between where they are and where they could be.

Think of our imperfect selling model, and how it maintains itself and how it has created work-arounds, blame, and push strategies to mitigate the abysmal close rate. It maintains its status quo because the system has deemed itself to be excellent, and has not been wiling to go through the change necessary, even at the risk of closing far fewer sales. I'll be discussing the system of sales in Chapter 7.

If we can help buyers walk through all of the elements of their status quo and discover an Identified Problem, we can guide them to discover how to address the elements that must change. But we cannot do this on the strength of our product details.

In fact, information doesn't teach someone how to make a decision. As we've seen, decisions get made on criteria. Too often, we assume that our pitch or presentation will offer just the right data to sway a purchase. That may be true—but only after the internal criteria are met and all systems are 'go.'

Often our prospects see the possibility of excellence. Sometimes, buyers need to maintain their status quo for reasons we cannot understand.

If buyers see nothing wrong, and we cannot facilitate their discovery that it's possible to have the system be even better, they will do nothing. One of the biggest flaws with sales is that we mistakenly try to convince prospects that they can be more effective with our solution when they are not certain of their criteria for change.

I once did training for a well-known spiritually-based leadership center. They were the most manipulative sales people I had ever met. No matter what I did, what I taught, they would add their new-found knowledge to their manipulation tactics.

One day I said to them, "Were you aware that you come off as being manipulative?"

One of them responded in surprise: "Of course we are! We have a right to be! People need our material!"

Ahhh. Moral authority!

CUSTOMERS DO KNOW HOW TO DECIDE

I offer a bit of caution here: It sometimes feels that we know more than our prospects, as they come up with seemingly inappropriate decisions, mislead us, and wait forever to make a seemingly obvious decision. I often hear the cry "Customers don't know how to decide." Of course they don't when they start. But we haven't had the tools to help them with the front-end of their decisions, either.

Neither buyers nor sellers know the route to excellence at the start of any change, and the sales model does not handle it. We're both flying blind and dependent on each other for excellence.

That is why David Sandler claimed that 'Buyers are Liars.' It isn't that they are dishonest. They just can't see the full range of systems issues that created and maintain their status quo.

A current prospect of mine was all ready to go with one of my solutions. He then disappeared off the face of the earth for three weeks. When he emerged he said that the tech team didn't know how to add my material to what they were doing and still have relevance. And no one called to talk it through. I had threatened the system and they went into lockdown mode.

When we only see a leaf, we defend our reality, separate from the alternate reality others may observe. When we are outside the system and can look across from the adjacent mountaintop, we can help buyers get some perspective and begin to understand the systems issues involved with change so they can move forward and resolve their need.

Rule 2

Until the prospect explores all obvious, familiar ways to find a solution without choosing a new vendor or product/service, they will make no decision to buy anything new.

The system will seek to resolve the Identified Problem with familiar resources before agreeing to an external/unfamiliar solution.

Corporations would prefer to not buy new solutions. Anything new will potentially create disruption, so they would much prefer to maintain the status quo or use familiar vendors. Whatever route they take must not only resolve their business problem, but do it in a way that's congruent with the system and leaves behind as little disruption as possible.

Anything that enters a system from outside will naturally create instability. It's imperative that clients manage their need with a solution that their system will easily adopt with a minimum of chaos.

Think about this while considering learning Buying Facilitation®:

What has stopped you until now from adding new sales skills to the ones you're using to give you more success?

Indeed, how long do you spend trying to fix your own personal problems before seeking help?

Buyers will try to use old software, call familiar vendors first, and talk with other departments to see if they can find a familiar solution rather than use something 'foreign.' Going 'outside' to an unknown vendor is the last thing they want to do and they will go to great lengths to make what is familiar workable.

CHANGE CREATES DISRUPTION

I once got a call from a client in a major Professional Services firm saying that all of the Senior Partners were working day and night to write a proposal to answer an RFP from a long-standing prospect they had never worked with. They were determined to get it right this time. The prospect had always used Arthur Anderson as their provider before now.

SDM: What is stopping them from using Arthur Anderson this time?

PARTNER: What?? I have no idea. I'll call you back.

He called me back an hour later. He'd called the prospect and asked them why they weren't using AA again. The answer: "We are using AA. We always use AA. We just needed a second bid."

My client and I put together a list of Facilitative Questions, and sent those in instead of a proposal. Six weeks later, they got a call back: When AA started to do the work, they were asked to address the questions my client and I wrote up. AA never responded. But the questions were vital and needed resolution for the client to be successful. Here are two of the questions:

How will you know when the implementation team is going off course and needs to bring additional decision members on the team?

At what point will the managers need to add additional resources to ensure their teams' buy-in to the proposed changes?

Since we were proposing the management of the system of change, and AA had no organized route through buy-in and implementation, they fired AA, and brought my client in to do an eight-figure contract. They never did write that proposal.

> If the system knew how to fix its problem with a solution that is already familiar, it would have done so already.

This element of a buying decision is actually the easiest. If the system knew how to fix its problem with a solution that is already familiar, it would have done so already. But they still have to consider all familiar possibilities before making a decision to consider a non-familiar 'fix'. Unfortunately for us, they sometimes are just beginning the process of systems agreement once they've already begun speaking with us.

The last resort is to bring in an unfamiliar fix from outside the system. But if the known, familiar resources will not produce the results they want, systems will be forced to seek an external solution and figure out how to manage the change.

Rule 3

Until or unless all elements of the systems that touch the Identified Problem have bought in to the new element entering the system, nothing will happen for fear of systems imbalance or systems disruption.

All systems elements that touch the Identified Problem must be willing to accept change and know how to collaborate with the change in order to maintain the integrity of the system.

Until all appropriate systems elements are included in a solution design, until the systems can figure out how to reassign staff, or get extra supervision, or shift job roles, there will be no decision to purchase a product or service.

To continue down your own route to discovery, here is a Facilitative Question:

How would you go about bringing in your boss and helping him/her discover how Buying Facilitation® would serve you and the team, prior to moving forward in your learning?

Systems elements include people, policies, initiatives, job descriptions, HR dictums, rules, fears, technology, work-arounds—whatever is touching the Identified Problem and managing the need until it gets resolved by a better solution.

This is the tactical part of the buying decision where sellers can show how smart they are. This is where I help prospects determine that the tech team should be involved, or one of the managers from a different department needs to be on the decision team. Remember that systems are so frightened of disruption that they need to ensure that all of the 'players' be involved, and each loose end be sewn up, before any money will be approved.

Because this is a complex issue, I've devoted all of Section Three to introducing the skills to help buyers encourage buy-in.

WHAT IS INVOLVED IN MANAGING CHANGE

Sometimes the issues that influence the buying decision are unconscious, or are historic, or are in other departments. Make no mistake: These elements must be discovered and managed before solutions are sought.

Here are the elements and people that must buy in, in order for a buying decision to take place:

1. The person directly responsible for the area holding the Identified Problem, and his/her superiors.

2. The people that work within the area that a solution will reside.

3. The people or technology that are providing a work-around for the Identified Problem.

4. All of the rules that have kept the status quo in place.

5. All of the initiatives that are working around and maintaining the Identified Problem.

6. All of the people and departments that will be affected by the change that the new solution will bring: technology (techies, techie managers, users), R&D, and the management folks who must buy in to the new solution, pay for it, manage it, and maintain it.

7. The budget: where will it come from; the accounting practices regarding how the project will be monetized and for how long; what has to be moved around.

8. Current vendor issues, including the relationships the buyers have had with vendors over time.

9. Wildcards: whatever other stakeholder, financial, technical, or people issues that need to be managed.

Disturbingly, the people who influence implementation, or who are tangled in the work-arounds may or may not be placed on the Buying Decision Team. Far too often, no one involves them until it's too late.

I once was good-to-go with a prospect and his sales team. We met, loved each other, had conference calls. They all read my ebook and were excited. I sent the prospect a contract, he signed it, and then sent it to his COO—who proceeded to hit the roof.

"You're paying WHAT for SALES TRAINING??"

My prospect had his own budget and was the regional director of sales. He answered to the CFO, not the COO. Enter a new stakeholder that hadn't been on the initial Buying Decision Team.

Thankfully I was able to use Facilitative Questions to teach him how to make a new decision—not based on price, but by helping him shift his beliefs about what training meant to him and his company. It had nothing to do with me or my offering.

> **If you want to read the transcript of this dialogue, go to www.newsalesparadigm.com/newsletters/moneyobjections**

I'll say it again (and again and again): Until or unless buyers figure out how to come up with their own best answers, they will do nothing. And the system will reject the attempts of anything new to get in without approval.

Conventional sales has now begun addressing the topic of buyer's buying decisions. But the model they are using merely addresses the area directly around the need and don't address the systems-change issues. I hope that with this book they'll add the offline change piece as well.

CHAPTER

CORPORATE CULTURES
IN TIMES OF RISK

[WHAT WE KNOW]

- In times of economic distress, buyers take longer to make decisions.

- Customarily reliable measurement tools are either not viable or produce unreliable data when the measured data are in flux.

- When job descriptions change and reorganizations take place, Buying Decision Teams shift and decision making is difficult.

[WHAT WE HAVEN'T KNOWN]

- By proving to be helpful at leading buyers through the maze of confusion going on, buyers will put us on their Buying Decision Team.

- Buyers can buy if the decision team knows how to mitigate their risk factors and agree to the criteria they will use to make decisions.

[WHY DOES IT MATTER]

■ Buyers will buy nothing now if they don't know how to manage or mitigate risk.

■ Sellers can lead buyers through their criteria and make themselves an important asset to the Buying Decision Team, thus differentiating you from your competition.

ECONOMIC MELTDOWNS such as the ones we faced 2000—2001, and again in 2009, cause confusion. Having the tools to facilitate buyers through their decisions will enable us to be seen as true servant leaders as well as bring in business. We can actually:

■ use our leadership skills and authenticity to build our client base during times of economic uncertainty;

■ show buyers how to make creative choices they may not have otherwise recognized;

■ teach buyers how to address all of the issues they need to manage;

■ become part of the Buying Decision Team as they go through change and free up funds; and

■ close a lot more business than we would have otherwise.

During times of economic stress, our clients still need to run a business. They must carry a brand, continue their initiatives, keep their customers, and make a profit. Yet corporate leaders too often prefer to maintain their status quo rather than take any new risks.

With our new understanding of the types of systems issues our buyers face when they experience 'need' in the area our product serves, we'll be in position to lead them through their confusion and have a competitive advantage.

KNOWING SYSTEMS CAN OFFER LEADERSHIP

Here is an example of understanding systems well enough to lead a buyer to their point of excellence.

In the field of sales training, I know

- that the internal training team needs to buy in to a new program;

- program participants must desire a new sales model, be willing to go through a two-month learning cycle, and be open to changing what they customarily do;

- current training vendors may need to work with me to align the new change with the old material;

- adjacent teams—marketing, web presence, customer service—may need to buy in to change or want to attend training;

- a pilot may be set up, with a control situation to monitor success;

- people will need to free up their budgets.

In my experience, the biggest systems problem buyers face is with the internal training group: Do they want to be involved? Buy a license? Sit in on the pilot? Perform after-program coaching? Change some of their current training programs to match the new material? Do they want to license my IP and design a program themselves?

Buyers need to know the answers to these questions. I can facilitate their decisions to make sure that they get the decision made quickly, but I can't make the decisions for them.

I can know what excellence looks like when a buyer is in a position to bring the elements together to make a new decision. I will never understand all of the details, the history, and the political climate that keeps the status quo in place—nor do I need to. But the buyer must.

My job is to lead my clients to each element they must include in order to succeed through the confusion. I do this by facilitating their decision-making first, then placing my product second.

Once we understand how to lead buyers to their best decisions, we will be seen as assets and be invited onto their Buying Decision Teams.

I'm not saying buyers will accept us onto their Buying Decison Teams automatically. But if we redefine our job descriptions as offering leadership and decision strategy, we'll have an easier time.

NEW DECISION FACTORS

To maintain homeostasis in times of economic confusion, companies face new types of decisions:

Risk Factors

- *Understand* what is at *risk* within the culture (money, positioning, people, time, competitive edge, vendors, initiatives, competition factors) *and* possible *fall out.*

- *Determine priorities:* what should be done now, what can wait.

- Consider how to *resolve* the economic, political, and resolution *issues* and *limit consequences.*

- *Decide* what systems elements are *essential:* staff? partners? outlets? product lines? Do we need to divest? Do we need to find a partner for an M&A?

- Recognize the *risk-reward* possibilities and probabilities: Do we act now, wait, shift the options? Do we dismantle current vendor relationships? Find new ones?

- *Agree on* tolerable levels and types *of failure* and how to manage the consequences.

- Determine the *risk* of *doing nothing.*

Financials

▪ Decide how to *manage income issues:* Do we strip
down? Lay off? Save? What do we spend money on?
Do we freeze all expenditures? Cut costs? Pay less?
Buy cheap? Spend now? What needs to be given a full
budget? Who decides?

▪ *Manage cash flow and pricing:* Do we keep all product
lines? Shift prices? Design new promotions? What are
the acceptable cash flow parameters?

▪ Decide what sort of a *cash position* we need to
maintain.

▪ Decide who makes decisions around *operating costs*
and how to manage them.

▪ Choose which, if any, *revenue projections* to show
stakeholders and shareholders.

Initiatives

▪ *Eschew innovation;* maintain core business and
practices.

▪ *Resolve immediate needs* that may have *economic*
or *political* repercussions and assess the consequences
of action/no action.

▪ *Do scenario planning:* What does the future look like?
What actions need to be taken? What teams will be
doing what, and with whom? How can we monitor
the outcomes or fallout?

▪ Group brainstorm: What are our *criteria for resolving*
new and historic plans and *initiatives? Determine
timing:* Do it now or later? Not at all? Or only when
a problem is pressing?

Human Capital

■ *Create leadership initiatives* to support shifting teams and personnel in order to foster trust, internal leadership, and team work.

■ Develop leadership initiatives to *design internal messaging* to *handle* the heightened *fears* of the employees. Must be informative, consistent, inclusive, recurrent, and have a strong leadership element that gives each employee the possibility of taking a leadership role.

■ *Personnel:* Who gets laid off? How do salaries get re-apportioned? How do we manage the remaining staff in order to retain work ethic.

Decisions still have to be made regardless of the economy. And although we can't be inside with them, we can at least have an understanding of the elements that need to be managed.

Note that when facing any financial risk, corporations have a responsibility to their shareholders to not spend money if they can save it. Therefore, unless you can enter their world with a decision facilitation strategy instead of a 'sales' strategy, you will face the following problems:

1. *Buyers will wait as long as they can to define a 'need'.* Until or unless they figure out that something is not 'fine,' and the gap between their status quo and excellence is too large to continue functioning optimally, they will do nothing.

2. *Buyers will develop as many work-arounds as possible. Their search for excellence will be reduced to the maintenance of the status quo.* Until or unless they recognize that their status quo is suboptimal, they will do nothing.

3. *Buyers will remain risk averse until they develop new cultural norms to guide their decision making. They will*

say: "Call back in six months," or "We're doing nothing now." Until buyers know how to make the right decisions in a way that maintains the values within the new culture, they will do nothing.

Times of economic stress are perfect opportunities for us to enter with our new job descriptions!

A VIEW OF INDIVIDUAL AND CORPORATE SYSTEMS

In times of corporate or economic stress, buyers go through some form of change management issues as they reconfigure their departments, lay off people, or put initiatives on hold. They must end what they are familiar with while their staff have motivation issues and polarized attitudes. Ultimately they must start over and become something different.

The change issues go on both within the personal level, as per each employee, and at the corporate level.

Individual

Let's start with the assumption that whatever role each individual played among their peers, whatever job description or political capital someone has held, has changed in some way. The members must reconfigure themselves around new members, layoffs, changes in corporate initiatives, options, relationships, and political capital.

In other words, the normal route folks have followed to make buying decisions is up for grabs. And new corporate mandates may be a daily occurrence.

People end up shifting roles in order to maintain professionalism in their work, especially when there is a possibility of people losing their jobs and being asked to work with new teams, new job descriptions or new mandates.

Individuals might change from being innovators and problem solvers to being seen as the 'responsible' one who maintains stability and group consensus. They might take on a leadership role, or halt innovation. Or they might sabotage new initiatives, or seek new job descriptions with new responsibilities.

Given that many people may be asked to work together in new teams, with no history, and few skills at managing internal and external crises together, achieving consensus may be difficult.

People may not be as creative, responsible, or willing to lead as they once were and there may be some who seek to sabotage the group or minimize their personal risk by laying low and not helping where they could really be useful.

Indeed, the leadership and skills they were known for may possibly be irrelevant:

- What skills must they adopt to fit within a new decision team? To help influence new decisions?

- How do they handle their feelings? Their loss of old job status and standing among colleagues? Their fears of losing their job or watching old friends be laid off?

- How do they do their jobs differently? Handle a new political climate and new decision issues?

- Are they willing to make a difference? Take a stand? Influence others? Will they garner the power to implement or innovate?

And it is highly likely that the HR group may not be managing these issues effectively given that the future consequences are unknowable. Many of the conventional HR initiatives have depended on commonly accepted work place practices; at times of stress, there may not be the type of creativity necessary to face the ever-changing landscape.

Corporate

Under such conditions of risk, uncertainty, and change, everyone has different theories about how to proceed, and works from disparate beliefs. People may have no history of working together or assumptions or norms in common. A new culture is evolving.

During major change, the future is truly a mystery and there are no stable criteria to work from because no one knows what success will look like.

Ordinarily, the company's internal structure—rules, politics, policies, relationship hierarchies, departmental configuration—is stable, so any disruption from change is contained to one department, or one initiative. But when the corporate structure is in disarray, the daily activities must be kept stable and any potential for risk must be minimized.

The first thing many companies do is to pull the plug on as much spending as makes sense and maintain the status quo the best they can. They may:

1. prolong decisions (after all, the status quo has 'worked' for a while);

2. maintain maintain maintain;

3. throw overboard everything that doesn't seem necessary;

4. seek quick 'wins' from inside, and end the use of funds or external support to resolve any problems;

5. restructure to preserve their best assets;

6. identify what seem to be the 'must win' battles and delay the rest;

7. seek M&A opportunities;

8. discover the valuation drivers and control the messaging.

> Knowing what excellence will look like, and knowing how to go about getting buy-in for change are two of the criteria for deciding whether or not to fix an Identified Problem.

How does the company continue to do business in these circumstances? How does a decision get made in an environment of "NO"? Who will take the lead to request change and risk their political capital? Who will come out as a true leader and fight for the change that needs to be made now? And how does everyone agree what needs to get done *now*?

When the business environment is in flux while it figures out what 'business as usual' will look like, buyers are stumped. Of course they have needs and goals and initiatives to pursue. But they don't know what excellence will look like and don't know how to go about getting buy-in for change—two of the criteria for deciding whether or not to fix an Identified Problem.

Ordinarily, companies manage their status quo daily by issuing expected, replicable, and dependable directives that

- create stability,

- support ongoing management decisions,

- chart success and failure, and

- manage and contain the current initiatives.

This is quite important: Under 'normal' economic conditions, corporations have systems in place that make it possible to make high level business decisions, to track success and failure, and determine risk and reward. But when the business environment is in flux, the status quo has been disturbed. Corporate leaders no longer know what to look for or track and they must expend time, energy, and human capital on creating conditions for safety until the business environment stabilizes.

THE CULTURE OF I DON'T KNOW

What happens in this confusion if buyers need to resolve an Identified Problem? To begin with, they have a difficult time choosing their decision criteria. Their definition of who they are may be in flux and they won't always know what needs to shift.

During times of recession, or inflation, or depression—especially when it's a global problem—everything is at a stand-still as companies try to contain the damage, minimize loss, and figure out the future. Using work-arounds will maintain the status quo until they have all agreed on a set of criteria for decision making.

Here are the issues they face:

- They are using work-arounds that may or may not be effective, but are 'good-enough' until they aren't. And only a fraction of the people know what is going on.

- They may be losing their jobs, or reorganizing, and working with new teammates.

- They are in new situations with new cultures, developing new norms that have no history and may or may not fit into their historic system.

- They either have to try to re-create their original system of rule and roles and relationships, or develop a new one; they don't yet have new systems elements, or history together, with which to recreate a new culture.

- They will either try to use the old rules, or develop new ones. Of course this will depend on the most senior people. But as outsiders, we won't know what's going on.

Essentially, there is a systems problem, with no certain way to reach a consensus, no historic criteria to base decisions on, and no new rules in place.

As we attempt to help these companies make decisions during these hard times, we must help them through their systems issues. This will allow us to get onto their Buying Decision Team, to be seen as true Trusted Advisors and Relationship Managers, and to be there when they are ready to make purchasing decisions.

Let's now go to the seller's environment, and see how all of these systems issues and decision issues are affecting us.

THE SELLER'S WORLD

It was six men of Indostan
To learning much inclined,
Who went to see the Elephant
(Though all of them were blind),
That each by observation
Might satisfy his mind.

The First approach'd the Elephant,
And happening to fall
Against his broad and sturdy side,
At once began to bawl:
"God bless me! but the Elephant
Is very like a wall!"

(continued on next page)

(continued from previous page)

The Second, feeling of the tusk,
Cried,—"Ho! what have we here
So very round and smooth and sharp?
To me 'tis mighty clear
This wonder of an Elephant
Is very like a spear!"

The Third approached the animal,
And happening to take
The squirming trunk within his hands,
Thus boldly up and spake:
"I see," quoth he, "the Elephant
Is very like a snake!"

The Fourth reached out his eager hand,
And felt about the knee.
"What most this wondrous beast is like
Is mighty plain," quoth he,
"'Tis clear enough the Elephant
Is very like a tree!"

The Fifth, who chanced to touch
        the ear,
Said: "E'en the blindest man
Can tell what this resembles most;
Deny the fact who can,
This marvel of an Elephant
Is very like a fan!"

The Sixth no sooner had begun
About the beast to grope,
Then, seizing on the swinging tail
That fell within his scope,
"I see," quoth he, "the Elephant
Is very like a rope!"

And so these men of Indostan
Disputed loud and long,
Each in his own opinion
Exceeding stiff and strong,
Though each was partly in the right,
And all were in the wrong!

MORAL.
So oft in theologic wars,
The disputants, I ween,
Rail on in utter ignorance
Of what each other mean,
And prate about an Elephant
Not one of them has seen!

—**John Godfrey Saxe's** (1816-1887)
version of the famous Indian legend

CHAPTER

HOW CAN WE SELL
TO HELP BUYERS BUY?

In this chapter, we'll unravel the 'system' of sales and see how we buy in to solution-focused sales. I'll introduce new beliefs, new goals, and new results that will match the new system of decision facilitation. Imagine understanding how to help buyers manage to buy faster and with integrity!

During the chapter:

■ We will examine the systems elements of our typical sales process;

■ We will recognize how the system has created our results;

■ We will discuss the new skills we must adopt to help buyers manage their decisions prior to a product purchase.

THE JOB OF merely placing product or service is over. We started out with Dale Carnegie and traditional sales, followed by Linda Richardson introducing us to consultative sales. Seth Godin gave us permission marketing. The internet has brought us Sales 2.0.

Thousands of sales books have been written, giving us new ideas and tactics to Help us Sell. Be Authentic. Get to the top. Find the Decision Maker. Go Around the Gatekeeper. Understand the buyer. Network. Get Face-to-Face. Overcome Objections. Strategizing. Relating. SPINning.

The above are all based on every way conceivable to influence, manipulate, and convince a buyer to make a purchase. These models have brought success. But we can be so much more successful once we add the front end support.

Since the inception of sales—when the serpent convinced Eve to eat the apple?—the job of facilitating the buyer's offline, idiosyncratic buying decision issues has not been part of the sales model.

I mentioned this capability to someone today. He said, "You're helping us take care of those people who hijack the sale," assuming that the seller is right, it's a battle to close, and the buyer is actively avoiding a purchasing decision.

In our daily lives, before we commit to any sort of expenditure or change, we must handle our feelings, our bosses, our spouses, our finances and…

As sellers, we become almost predatory and single focused.

As sellers we have been like the blind men in the poem: We see the parts that are in front of us, and then call the buyer stupid when their decisions are based on parts we can't see, and they don't make the decisions we think they should.

As a result we've been less successful than we should have been, and have served our clients less than we could have.

A NEW SALES MODEL FOR A NEW ERA

Our economy, the global issues, and the internet, are all creating new buyers who are developing better and better work-arounds for the problems our products can resolve. Making a product purchase to solve a business problem is less likely than ever before. Plus, a product or service sale that follows our accustomed time/relationship trajectories is unlikely. It's said that it's taking 50% longer to close a sale now.

As the representatives of our companies, with great knowledge of the system and subject matter our solution handles, we are uniquely positioned to serve our buyers. We know our market, our demographics, and our buyer's preferences. We know our competition and how they differentiate themselves from us—and how we must position ourselves to differentiate from them. We understand the 'needs' element of the issues our buyers face, and how our solution can serve them.

Before now, we were in service to a sale. Now we must first be in service to our clients. We have no choice; managing just the solution end isn't enough to close even the numbers we're used to closing. Buyers need more than a new solution; uncovering or managing need isn't enough.

With our new beliefs, our new skills, our new understanding of how to help people discover their own best answers we are uniquely situated to enable prospects to attain excellence.

Let's discover how. Take note: *The sales system, similar to a buyer's system, is a self-perpetuating system that will fight change.*

THE SYSTEM OF SALES

The sales system is designed to place product. We buy into it, we believe it, we defend it, we make it our own—failed sales and all.

We can call it anything we want—managing need, caring for our customers—but net/net, it's about selling something. Because the system has left out an offline part of the equation, we've resorted to work-arounds that have become accepted parts of the system, and have reduced our success as well.

I'm going to name some conventionally used sales tools that are actually work-arounds—necessary because we've asked buyers to make solution choices too early in their decision cycle:

■ *money objections:* When buyers don't yet understand how to value their need or how a new solution will reconfigure the current system, they will not understand how much they are willing to pay for a solution (Note: This has nothing to do with the value of our solutions.).

■ *handling gatekeepers:* When folks who protect our prospects know how to choose to put us through, they won't need to be influenced in any way—it's their job to find the folks their bosses need to speak with.

■ *closing techniques:* Once buyers have their buying criteria in place, and have gotten buy-in from the Buying Decision Team, they will know what steps they need to take to close themselves.

■ *relationship management:* We have assumed that 'making nice' would help us close a sale. Buyers will choose the solution that best matches their buying criteria. If there are similar solutions, they will choose the person who has helped them facilitate their decisions.

■ *making appointments:* Dale Carnegie taught us to get in front of people. That was in 1937, and that was when it was imperative to show people your solution in person. Now we have websites, and the internet and conference calls. Not to mention it's possible to use Buying Facilitation® on the phone. Once we help the buyer figure out how to put together the whole Buying Decision Team, we can visit once the team is on board. [Note: I jokingly say, "Don't use your body as a prospecting tool."]

■ *nurture marketing:* Because we have been pushing product, we have learned ways to keep hammering at the buyer, assuming that if we make nine connections, they'll finally buy from us. Right.

- *influencing/convincing strategies:* Because we've been pushing in to a closed system, and concentrating on placing a solution at the wrong end of the buying decision sequence, we've found ways to 'get in.' Once we can help buyers figure out what they need to figure out internally, there is no need to convince or influence. Remember: These tactics only work less than 10% of the time.

If, when meeting a buyer for the first time, we assume that s/he is in need of a solution NOW, and enter the sales process assuming that our solution might be chosen, we create resistance and lost sales. We then complain of the time wastage, the objections we have to manage, the difficulty closing—problems that occur because we enter at the wrong time, in the wrong context, with the wrong skill set and don't manage the buyer's full set of buy-in needs.

Here are the aspects of a sales system.

Language: Because the goal is to place product, and because we unwittingly focus on the last steps of the buying process before the buyer has completed their first steps, the sales language focuses on finding ways to defend and deny the reactions of buyers. So we 'push into', 'get in', or 'go around' by 'understanding need' or placing product and developing 'relationships'. Many terms are warlike or based on deception—'battle', 'guerrilla', 'nailed', 'smoke screen', 'lying', 'pain', 'overcoming', 'convince'—because sales has become a competition against the buyer.

Sellers also use a lot of storytelling to get commiseration on lost sales, so they get 'hijacked' and 'raided,' thereby maintaining their expected failure.

Because of the pervasive history of high failure rates (the relative time-to-success equation is out of whack because we ignore the off-line decisioning), we tell each other similar stories: in our stories, our buyers lie, make stupid decisions, don't tell the truth, forcing sellers to work around, go above, push and convince.

The expectation of failure is universally accepted by the sales community and it's reinforced in coded language patterns. We knowingly shake our heads in commiseration as we hear an expected story of what a dumb thing a buyer did. Indeed, the language patterns help perpetuate the failure of the system. Hence, when Buying Facilitation® has been trialed, and has been proven over and over again, over 20 years and across industries and countries, to bring in results that are 200—800% more successful than the 'sales' model, I'm told that I'm lying.

Sales has not had a vocabulary to enable a discussion around facilitating a buyer's off-line, internal, unique, subjective, and human, systemic change issues.

To change the system we need:

- *new languaging:* facilitate change; engage buying decisions team; get on to the Buying Decision Team early; buy-in; decision facilitation; Buying Facilitation®; no objections or pricing problems;

- *new stories:* we closed in weeks/months; the whole Buying Decision Team was at our first meeting; they never discussed price; we were able to close without a price discussion; there were no competitors.

Customs, Traditions, Rituals: Because of the focus on push *into*, and the failures that result when a system defends itself, the conventional sales practices implicitly assume failure. I recently saw a blog that asked 'experts' "If you got a new lead would you 'pounce', 'wait', or 'nurture'" These choices were based on two underlying convictions: 1. the buyer is prey and a 'thing' to be managed in some way, and 2. if the seller knew how to do it 'just right' the buyer would buy.

All sales rituals and customs are built upon the push, the discovery, the persuasion so the seller can find the best route 'in.'

One more important fact: Because we have a +/- 10% success rate, we build in these low numbers to commission payments and hiring practices. We hire nine times more people to make up the difference, pay according to a 90% failure rate, and accept that our sales folks will be 'wasting' 90% of their time. *And then we pay sellers more than anyone else because they need battle pay for all of the rejection they get!*

To change the system:

■ *expect a 40% close rate; hire half the normal sales staff; use half the travel expenses; understand systems; focus only on systemic buy-in and change management; and use decision phases to help buyers decide on vendor issues, work-arounds, budget, timing, buy-in.*

Politics, Policies: All politics are built around placing product: wait for buyer to return or find a way around the prospect; find an inside influencer; follow-up, and follow up and follow up; make appointments; present, pitch, brand; use manipulation and influencer strategies to encourage trust and relationships; and manage call reluctance—all in service to managing a need we think we have control over.

We are outsiders, pushing in to an unfamiliar system and then blaming the system for not allowing us in—rather than teaching the system to open and change.

To change the system:

■ *sellers and buyers together determine meetings and conversation topics; buyers trust sellers to be external consultants and aren't focused on placing a solution; sellers are responsible for helping buyers bring together the right people quickly; sellers support the decision process and are judged for these skills first before being judged on product.*

Relationships: Sellers, believing that they will be chosen if the buyer likes or trusts them more, build relationships on 'understanding need' and 'making nice' and being a Trusted Advisor so the buyer will favor them over their competitors.

None of this has any validity in fact, or more sales would close. Early decision issues may or may not confirm a need and may have nothing to do with a solution choice.

Buyers buy when they get buy-in from their system and know how to change without harming the system. Period. If the decision is to find an external solution, and solutions are similar, then relationships win out.

To change the system:

■ *sellers help buyers facilitate their decisions before discussing need or solution; act as neutral navigators, and build relationships based on trust and servant leadership.*

Rules, Assumptions, Values: Our focus on selling a solution and believing that we know what buyers need, maintains faulty assumptions:

■ If a solution is presented appropriately, if the buyer likes and trusts you, and the buyer's need fits your solution, then the buyer is a hot prospect. If they don't buy, they are stupid.

■ Buyers buy emotionally (which is assumed because buyers behaviors have been incomprehensible to the seller).

■ If the buyer gets the right information about the solution, the information will help them decide.

■ Sales take X amount of time (as per industry standard) to close.

■ Buyers know what sort of solution they need.

- When a buyer contacts a seller, s/he wants to resolve a need.

- Buyers are liars (first said by David Sandler in the '80s because buyers weren't aware of what they didn't know, and they defended themselves against sellers).

- Dealing with top decision makers will make the sale.

- Be aware of who makes the decisions.

- Price is important and must be competitive.

- Face-to-face visits will help sell because it creates relationships.

The low success rate that accompanies these assumptions raises the obvious question of why they have persisted. Indeed, why has sales been so successful at avoiding change?

To change the system, sellers must now assume:

- *The seller's job is to help the buyer change in a non-disruptive way.*

- *Buyers buy when their system buys in to change.*

- *Product information is the last thing buyers need.*

- *Sales cycles are a function of the buying decisions.*

- *At first contact, the sales job is to lead the buyer down the decision funnel.*

- *Buyers don't lie and offer the best available data they have at the time.*

- *The whole decision team chooses a solution.*

- *Price is only an issue if a buyer can't decide between two equal things.*

- *Face-to-face is necessary only when the whole decision team determines it needs to see the seller.*

SPECIOUS ASSUMPTIONS

With basic assumptions that are largely irrelevant to our buyer's buying patterns, we end up unwittingly asking the wrong questions, gathering the wrong data at the wrong time, and ignoring some crucial bits that we always discover much later on.

We don't even consider that, at first contact, buyers have not fully defined their 'need,' are in their early stages of internal discovery and criteria alignment, and prefer to find ways to solve problems with internal or familiar resources.

We have designed a failed system that manages only a small part of a buying decision. We end up blaming buyers, blaming products, blaming marketing efforts, blaming ourselves—and we never blame the sales model. Instead we work harder and harder to push better and better using the same failed approach, getting the same results.

This is why buyers seem so stupid: We are focusing on the need, the pain, the solution, the price. They are focusing on maintaining systems integrity. Of course, when it's time to discuss, and possibly place, our solution, we need to understand exactly what the 'need' is. But we have other work to do first.

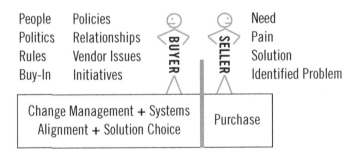

Solving the buyer's Identified Problem with our solution requires a different skill set than the one we must use to help them get buy-in to change.

SALES DOES NOT ADDRESS OFF-LINE DECISIONS

Sales places so much influence on 'understanding' a 'need' so we can place our solution. Here is what we are doing when we gather information and work so hard on understanding the need:

1. We can understand the Identified Problem, and the full set of needs—in relation to our solution.

   We have disregarded the internal issues buyers have to address and that bias their solution choice.

2. We can understand how the lack of a solution has affected buyers in relation to the area directly around the Identified Problem, not in relation to the rest of their culture.

   We have no understanding of the history or ongoing systemic repercussions of the problem, the rules and relationships that maintain it, or the work-arounds that manage it.

3. We can understand how our solution will help buyers to solve their problem at the point of 'need'.

   We have no way of knowing what internal change issues might occur, and need to be prevented, when buyers consider bringing in a new solution.

4. We know how to handle objections, develop relationships, and create 'value' in relation to placing our product.

   We don't have skills to facilitate decisions, maneuver through hidden systems, help buyers manage change.

5. If we're good, we even understand the ramifications of our solution—in relation to the defined 'need.'

   When buyers begin their discovery process, they don't know the sorts of problems they'll encounter on their way to buy-in, and we have had no means to guide them through that process.

ADDING NEW TASKS TO MANAGE SYSTEMS

Our new job is to lead buyers through their full range of decision factors. If we go back to you (the reader) figuring out if you want to learn Buying Facilitation®, you'd be helping your boss and your colleagues figure out their criteria around working with you while you use a different selling model; you'd be asking yourself Facilitative Questions to understand the changes you're willing to make and the internal risks you'd have to manage. We'll get into more of the specifics in Section Three.

For now, let's just make sure we buy in to our new roles as leaders. We will now:

1. facilitate collaboration in stakeholder teams and encourage authenticity, shared values, and flexibility;

2. lead decision teams to uncover problematic issues and begin to do some scenario planning;

3. help decision teams establish their criteria for success and failure based on their shared values;

4. help decision teams choose solutions that will enter their systems without disruption;

5. lead teams through discovering how they can resolve the problem themselves using familiar resources, even if it means helping them choose a competitor (if the competitor is their familiar vendor already);

6. help teams know when/if it is time to bring in a new solution partner;

7. help teams determine the best solution and best solution partner;

8. help teams manage integration so new solutions will align with values and current practices.

Buyers need help making the necessary decisions to move forward with some degree of certainty. They have to figure this all out anyway—with us or without us. With us, the sales model expands to include the change management, decision facilitation, servant leadership, and true consulting to close more sales. Quickly. And we're in integrity with our buyers.

CHAPTER NINE

HOW DECISION FACILITATION WORKS: AN OVERVIEW

In this chapter, I'll review a recent prospecting scenario to give you an overview of Buying Facilitation®. We'll get into far more depth in Section Three.

During the chapter:

- We will learn how buyers enter their buying decision process with little understanding of how to manage the gap between the perceived problem and the issues they need to address to move forward;

- We will be introduced to the new skills necessary to facilitate buying decisions;

- We will understand how to use Facilitative Questions;

- We will recognize the huge time savings in the sales cycle once buyers maneuver efficiently through their off-line discovery process;

- We will see how easy it is to facilitate change decisions, get onto the Buying Decision Team, and have a huge influence on the course of the buying decision process despite having little understanding of the 'need'.

TO SHOW YOU the differences between sales—the solution-placement end of the call that you're accustomed to—and the new decision facilitation component, I'm going to relate a recent prospecting situation.

FACILITATIVE QUESTIONS MANAGE THE BUYING DECISION PROCESS

Let me begin by formally introducing you to Facilitative Questions. I developed Facilitative Questions when I read the early books of Roger Schank and learned that information is stored in the brain in indices and recalled with questions. This got me thinking: How did the brain know where to look to make sure it got the best data to make decisions with? And what sort of data was necessary to make value-based decisions?

Playing around with those thoughts, I came up with the Facilitative Question: It grabs data from different parts of the brain (that the brain might not do automatically) and brings the data together so the person has the full range of appropriate criteria to consider. These questions are almost opposite to typical sales questions that gather data.

Typical questions ask about a decision that's already been made. One of the problems with these questions is that the buyer is very close to the issue, looking at the leaf, with no ability to have perspective. They know the answers, and the questions do not instigate change. Not to mention that the answers they will have at the beginning of their discovery process are not the same answers they'll have once they are ready to make a purchase.

A simple, typical information-based question would be:

Why do you wear your hair like that?

Facilitative Questions move the person to the mountaintop, forcing her to consider all relevant issues (some she may have overlooked, some she would discover later) such as timing considerations, stakeholder criteria, personality or departmental issues, the ability to change. Using the above simple question as the model, here's an example of a Facilitative Question:

How would you know if it were time to reconsider your hairstyle?

Note that it directs thinking to taking an action, considering time, considering choice, and considering personal issues. Try it out on yourself.

Facilitative Questions help your buyers recognize possibility and manage the sometimes unknown systems issues they need to address off-line. (Remember that at the beginning of their process, buyers don't know their route to a buying decision.)

They actually direct the buyer's thinking process and help them go sequentially through each aspect of the decisions they need to tackle (see page 73), down a route that will lead them to answers. Like an OD consultant would lead a company through change, or a coach would lead a client, they actually teach the buyer how to get systems buy-in and willingness to change.

I do not use them to manipulate a sale or gather data to make a pitch. Using these I do not need to be a part of the system or even understand details or nuances that I'm not privy to.

Facilitative Questions are the main skill in Buying Facilitation®. Indeed, we are helping the buyer figure out how to buy congruently.

Using these will give you skills of a real Trusted Advisor, help you close business much, much faster, find more prospects, and get on the buyer's Buying Decision Team.

Here are some situations that Facilitative Questions manage.

1. If buyers have an Identified Problem, it's most probably being managed by some familiar/internal resource that has been operational for a period of time and gives them some level of success. So the status quo—although sub optimal—is good enough.

Question: How will they know if maintaining their status quo is creating more vulnerability than they recognize? How will they know when the internal resource needs to be supplemented with additional resources?

2. If buyers are in dire need of new options, they will most likely enhance what they are already doing, purchase a partial solution or use something cheap, rather than make any costly changes that will require people/policy/technology/time costs.

Question: How will they know if the solution they seek would be best served with a partial, cheaper solution, or with modified internal resources? At what point would they recognize the need to add resource to what they already have?

3. If they have no idea the range of possibility of success, they have no idea how to choose one solution over another, and will make no choices.

Question: How will they know when it's time to take a risk on making a purchase? What is the fallout if all expenditures are on hold?

4. If buyers have no idea of how the new people-systems are operating, they don't know the fallout to bringing in a new solution, and may choose to do nothing until this is resolved.

Question: How do choices get made when fallout is unknown? How does the decision team factor in confusion?

5. If buyers have no way of knowing the range of issues they need to manage, they will push back on doing anything that will cause disruption.

Question: How will they involve the right people and initiatives?

Now we're beginning to get the hang of this new job of maneuvering buyers down their decision making process. Let's see how it applies.

INTRODUCTION TO A FACILITATED PROSPECTING SITUATION

As you read the scenario below, notice how I am putting together everything we've learned: systems thinking, decision facilitation, Facilitative Questions, and my constant focus on helping the buyer recognize and address the necessary systems elements so he can move forward. As you'll see, before they can even consider my solution, they have a change management problem.

> This is quite different from what you're used to; there is no pitch, no data gathering, no understanding of needs, no protracted discussion of needs.

Notice how the call is progressed without me having much data about the Identified Problem. This is quite different from what you're used to; there is no pitch, no data gathering, no understanding of needs, no protracted discussion of needs. I will do that once the buyers have recognized how, or if, they are going to move forward.

Remember that in the early stages of a prospective buying situation, buyers won't know all they eventually need to know, so gathering data about 'need' is premature. But with my understanding of systems I can recognize if my prospect is going down the right path or needs direction. I can then use my questioning skills to help them through the initial discovery to make sure that all decision makers are on board, all vital considerations are on the table, and any problem areas are recognized early on.

Then the buyers will know what needs to happen for them to be ready and willing to go through change, and I'll know in a very short time if I have a prospect.

My intention on the first call is to

- have us both decide if moving forward makes sense,

- have us both recognize if their system is willing and able to go through change,

- have me determine if I want the work,

- have them discover the appropriate elements that belong in the decision to change or make a purchase,

- make sure that they get their Buying Decision Team together for our second contact.

To give you some perspective in relation to a typical sale, notice what I achieved in five days: I had an initial call with a new prospect, one brief tactics meeting, and one phone conference with six of the most senior people in one of the largest brokerage houses in the world. Here's what happened.

One Monday morning, I got a call from Sam, the head of client services at a globally recognized brokerage house. He had just signed a contract for his internal tech team to develop a $500,000 software tool that would enable their brokers to take better care of client needs while differentiating themselves from the competition.

After reading one of my books, Sam realized the new software didn't address the personal, subjective end of the buyer's buying decision. Could I help? Could I design some software or questionnaires to help buyers make good choices, and understand to choose this brokerage house over the competition?

On our initial call, I got a quick overview of his problem and determined that it would be fun work. Almost immediately, I changed the conversation from Sam asking me if I could help him to facilitating what I knew he'd need to address before he would be ready to make any purchasing decisions.

I can't wait to hear about the program you're designing. But before we do that, do you mind if I ask you some questions?

I knew that on our first call Sam couldn't know the full set of details of his Identified Problem, or what to do with the details of my solution until he had put together a full Buying Decision Team and they understood the issues.

My initial criterion on this first call was to get Sam to begin thinking about getting the right people onto the Buying Decision Team, get their initial discovery and decision making elements addressed, and get me a place on the team.

With the knowledge of how choices get made in large corporations that use my solution, and what excellence should look like regarding how people work together, I led Sam through the first two of the three decision phases as discussed in Chapter 5 (Where are you/what's missing, How can you fix the problem with internal resources). The third decision phase couldn't be addressed until the whole decision team was on board.

As I began facilitating Sam's choices and leading him from the leaf to the mountaintop, he realized that he hadn't accounted for at least one important aspects of his initiative: Due to a problematic installation and the resultant failure of an earlier initiative, Sam might have trouble getting buy-in from senior management and needed to add other stakeholders to the Buying Decision Team.

At my suggestion, Sam also invited the tech manager to the meeting. Knowing systems as well as I do, I know that tech groups hate having vendors come in to do the work they want to do. This potential problem was going to have to be addressed sooner rather than later, and I wanted to know immediately if there was going to be a problem here.

Once Sam recognized the people who needed to be on the Buying Decision Team, he scheduled a phone conference that included everyone for the Friday after our initial call. Sam and I had one other 15-minute call in between to discuss tactics.

Just as the conference call was starting, a visitor joined whom Sam hadn't expected: The big boss. "After I got the memo that you'd all be on this call, I thought I'd see what you were all up to. After all, you all report to me and I'm going to find out about this sooner or later." Oops. Or Cool. No way to know which.

UNDERSTANDING A NEED ISN'T ENOUGH

I used my knowledge of systems and change management to lead them through the types of issues they would have to consider: What had stopped them from doing the front-end portion of the project themselves? How did they know that adding something would give them what they were seeking? Were they willing to work with other colleagues who were not in their departments? How would this new initiative affect their work schedules? What would need to be involved to insure success?

As we all went down the list of buying decision issues, Sam began coming up with opposition from the boss regarding the problematic installation. He asked the group how we thought he should handle this. I used some Facilitative Questions to help them decide:

What will need to happen for you to manage that issue so you can move forward?

How will you know that the historic issue can teach us how to avoid the same problem as we move forward?

They were able to get pretty far through their decision stage. They began to create a complete picture of their status quo (which none of them had individually), recognize what was missing to achieve excellence, and consider if they needed the training team to develop a quick learning module.

Midway through the call I was asked to discuss my solution. I did so in about 10 seconds and then linked it back to the next decision they needed to make:

*I have developed a decision facilitation model called
Buying Facilitation® that can help your customers make
buying decisions very quickly. How will you know that
adding a front-end program will work well with your
proposed initiative?*

During the phone conference the boss was a 'Nay Sayer.' He
kept adding 'worst case' scenarios. Knowing that the boss needed to
make a business case to approve of my prospect's initiative, I used
my knowledge of systems to help him see a route through the pit-
falls. But I was really flying blind because as the call progressed,
Sam's solution need became far more complex:

*So I hear you saying that that didn't work well for you.
In order to avoid X, if we do Y when we start, you should
be able to achieve Z, right? What would the team need to
be considering now in order to give us a chance to make
Y happen effectively?*

*It sounds like your experience was the result of inadequate
management supervision and that if we decide to go
forward, we should build in a solution so we don't face
the same problem. How could the managers be brought
in early enough to ensure they bought in to success?*

Once I figured out how to manage the big boss, I had another
issue to deal with: As the familiar resource (Stage Two: How can
you fix the problem with your familiar resources?), the tech team
wanted to do the entire project and didn't understand why I was
necessary.

THE BUYING DECISION TEAM

I had seen this situation countless times. Tech teams need help letting others in sometimes; using a Facilitative Question can help
everyone make a decision here.

If I was going to be hired, it would be because the tech team would either let me work with them, or they would agree to hand the project over. Or, the boss would use company politics to get them to step away. In any case, they were my competition.

This is an important point to remember. The internal resource is always our main competitor since the systems seek homeostasis. The only chance I had for a job was if the Buying Decision Team would reject the tech team.

I did the best I could with a few Facilitative Questions:

How would you know if you could learn my material and do all of the tech work yourself?

At what point would you be ready to fit into Sam's time line and ensure the backend system would be ready in time?

What would you need to know from me to recognize if we could work together on this so you could learn my model, and be able to do it on your own the next time?

I know I was helping my competitor get work. But the team had to discuss this with them off-line anyway. I wanted to address it when we were all together so I'd possibly have some control over the way it was being considered.

Eventually, as I kept the folks comparing and deciding and choosing, and as I led them through new insights and choices and potential problems, Sam's teammates began making comments about how my 'great questions' were making them think, and they began asking for my advice.

Since no one had considered some of the possibilities before, nor understood what the changes would entail for each of them, we became a brainstorming group, sharing opinions and fears and creative possibilities.

We ended up with a long To-Do list—things that had to be resourced, searched, chosen—which we divided up. None of the to-dos could have been predicted before we started.

The uninvited visitor turned out to be an asset: His questions were valid and brought in issues we would have come up against later—when I wouldn't be there. Not to mention that this man held the power. If we hadn't handled his fears when we did, he would have refused to approve the project.

At the end of the conversation he said, "Good work, Sharon Drew. I would never have seen a way to resolve these issues, and would have never agreed to this. Thanks for showing us it's possible to have success here."

By the time we set our next appointment, I was firmly on the decision team. But make no mistake: I still have no way of knowing what the outcome will be because there are too many variables. And I am not there with them. I hope I can get Sam to take my lead by using some of my Facilitative Questions to pose to everyone. This is the best I can do from outside.

Ultimately, as a result of the 60 minute conference call, I moved the sale forward by approximately six months (that's a conservative estimate) and am almost assured of agreement from the whole team *if they decide to use an external vendor.*

I can tell you that if I were using conventional sales techniques, I would have used the first call as a 'buying query,' and gathered data to help me write up a proposal with time lines, staffing, pricing. I would have sent it off to my client who would have kept it on his desk until he had time to go through it and think about it. Eventually he'd give it to his boss, who would then have plenty of objections because of the unresolved historic problem, not to mention that the tech team would be the preferred vendor.

And it all would have died, months later.

The way it is now, I've got a firm place on the Buying Decision Team and am being kept in the loop by emails. Am I there for all of the off-line decisions? Absolutely not. But I'm in the loop. The last communication I had from Sam was a request for a few Facilitative Questions to help him with some stakeholders.

Here is what I accomplished within a week of first being contacted by my prospect:

- Group leaders not initially a part of the decision, were included in the Buying Decision Team.

- Participants developed into a group.

- Participants put together a to-do list and time line, including me in the equation.

- The group discovered past failures within the corporation, and the means to correct them.

- The top boss gave approval to move forward.

- I became part of the Buying Decision Team.

- I helped influence the choice of vendor, helping the team see the difference between using an 'external vendor' and using the internal one.

Still open: Will the tech team try to take over the whole project—and subsume my piece of it? Can the training team design a new program in time for a timely roll out? Will the other department heads lend a hand like they said they would? These issues would have come up anyway. Now they are coming up with me being a part of the decision, and much earlier so I don't waste months of time presenting, following up, and waiting. Plus I've helped the buyer move forward quickly toward his own goals.

SALES IGNORES THE BUYER'S MOST IMPORTANT NEED

In the story above, I had no idea what Sam's personal or historic departmental relationships were, or what the follow-on conversations would be after I hung up the phone. I didn't know what they'd end up buying from me. Frankly, with so many variables, I can't really understand what their 'need' will end up being.

I trust that once they decide what they'd have to figure out—unknowable at the early stages here, and possibly different from what my prospect had initially wanted—and use me to help them think and make good decisions, they should be able to make the decisions needed to purchase a solution. And *then* I can do my sales job.

CHAPTER

THE TEN STEPS OF A BUYING DECISION

In this chapter we'll introduce the ten steps of a buying decision.

During the chapter:

- We will learn the ten steps that all buying decisions must include;
- We will learn the unspoken rules of a buying decision.

AS WE NOW KNOW, buyers don't buy based on need, vendor relationships, budgeted expenditures, solution attributes or initiatives. They buy when their system is ready to bring in something new that will help them be excellent, with a minimum of disruption.

Our new job is to help buyers navigate through their systems, manage all of their internal chaos and change, untangle their work-arounds, and enable their buy-in so they can solve their business problem with our solution.

We will now play an influential role in helping buyers maneuver down the first half—the offline portion—of the decision cycle. Let's look at the specifics of what buyers must handle off-line so we'll have a sound understanding of how their system works.

BUYING CONSIDERATIONS

Here are the tasks that need to be accomplished and how we can influence them:

1. *Until buyers learn how to gather the right people together to collaborate, decide together, and take to action together, all else is moot.*

The Identified Problem lives in one department, but folks on the Buying Decision Team may be on disparate teams.

By helping buyers facilitate collaboration within their entire Buying Decision Team, there is a greater likelihood of a quick decision to act. Certainly the ultimate action might not be the one we would prefer. But there is a likelihood that once the decision team recognizes their criteria and enumerates the issues they must resolve, purchasing our product might be a high priority for them.

2. *Until buyers figure out what immediate needs in their environment must be addressed—whatever that means to them—they will not consider an external solution.*

Addressing 'immediate needs' might include solutions that are not in our area of expertise or that are actually competitive with our solution. The problem might be resolved with a creative or temporary solution rather than a product purchase. It might mean doing nothing until next quarter.

Until the Buying Decision Team recognizes and agrees to their immediate and mid-range goals, and to issues that need to be handled outside the direct path of the need—solution, they will not consider taking action regardless of how pressing their need or how impressive our solution.

If we can help buyers actually figure out their immediate problem areas and their most essential criteria they need to focus on, we will be seen as coaches and leaders, and be invited in to their decision teams. Not to mention being the first vendor they will connect with once they decide to purchase a product.

We might even show them how to manage their internal decision elements more efficiently than they could do on their own, and make a purchase a lot sooner.

> 3. *Until the buyer's familiar resources are proven to be ineffective, no action will be taken.*

We are accustomed to attempting to place our product when a client need seems to be a fit. Now we know that until they have tried to fix their own problem first, they won't purchase our solution.

When we first meet clients, we don't know how or if they have tried to fix the problem already.

One of the first things we must do is to help them determine if they can use a familiar resource for the fix: Can they fix the problem with their own internal group? Can they use their regular vendor?

I know it's difficult to try to give potential business away. We can either help clients determine whether they can resolve the problem on their own, or we can sit and wait until they call us back: They have to go through this process anyway, with us or without us.

Don't worry, though. Most probably, if an internal solution would have worked, it would have been tried already. Pointing them in this direction as a way to be of service will 'up' your 'street cred.'

> 4. *Until the entire Buying Decision Team recognizes that it would make economic sense to resolve their Identified Problem now with an external solution, no action will be taken.*

Buyers have been resolving their Identified Problem with a work-around until now and there is a case to be made for continuing the status quo until the economy stabilizes. But if we can help the decision team evaluate the difference between the cost (time, people, political, organizational) of continuing current practices versus the cost of bringing in a new solution and the stress to their culture, we will become part of the Buying Decision Team.

If costs can be seen in a way that overrides their economic concerns and leaves them better off, clients will make a purchase. We can help them appraise the full range of systemic 'givens' and include the human systems as well as the financial and tactical ones.

5. *Until the decision team recognizes all of the elements that touch the Identified Problem and keep it in place, they will take no action.*

Many of the buyer's work-arounds are not easily visible, or the stakeholders are in other departments, or old rules make change difficult. Whatever needs to happen to get buy in, to determine change issues, to agree on what excellence will look like is the length of the buying decision. We have never been a part of those sorts of decisions before. Now we can have some influence over them.

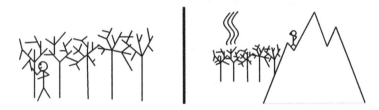

When we meet our prospects, they are seeing only the leaf of one tree—i.e. the most obvious aspect of their 'need'—in a forest in which the Identified Problem is merely a branch. That's one of the reasons that buyers don't give us all of the data we (and they) eventually need: they don't have it.

As sales people, we have abetted the problem by getting alongside of them and focusing on the same leaf.

It's time for us not only to understand the bigger picture, but also to lead our buyers to a place where they can see the bigger picture also, without the pull of ego, or job description, or bias.

Just think of it as two different jobs: First, get the Buying Decision Team on the route to discovery, buy-in, and collaborative decisions (Buying Facilitation®); second, offer them the solution that will make them excellent (sales).

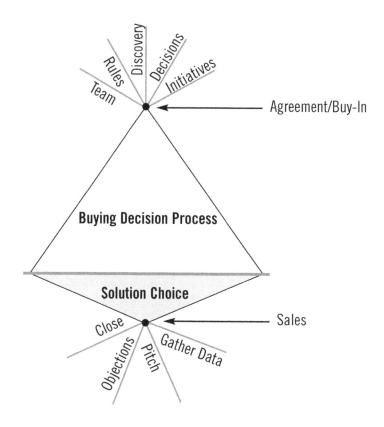

One of our most important jobs is to get the buyer to the mountain top to objectively see the complete picture that includes stakeholders, initiatives and outdated rules, and so on, and realize what it will take to create the environment in which change can occur. Together we can discover their next steps.

Because we will now be focusing on leading a buyer through their own decision issues rather than leading them to purchase our solution, it's imperative that we start off as impartial observers and focus on the system rather than the perceived need.

Remember that buyers have a bias around maintaining their system and will defend it if pushed. If they can gain the perspective and organize internally so that change won't be devastating, they will prefer excellence.

It's the same thing I have been doing with you at different points in the book: Knowing that your sales skills have been comfortable for so long, I've used Facilitative Questions to help you manage your discomfort around change. I've highlighted issues with your boss and teammates and your own tolerance for change and risk.

Until the entire range of possibilities (on the upside as well as the downside, and for all elements in the system) is visible and understood, there is no way to be in a position to consider the ramifications of change.

From the viewpoint of a leaf, all seems well, or at least manageable. From the mountain top, with no bias and a full view, it's possible to see adjacent problems and impediments to success, and recognize a need for change.

WHO IS A BUYER?

Since sales began, we've been taught that if we can answer the following questions, we've got a good chance of turning a prospect into a buyer:

1. Does that prospect's pain match your solution?

2. Is the prospect seeking a solution that your product or service can resolve?

3. Is the prospect on track to consider buying in a specific time scale?

4. Is the prospect a decision maker with functional responsibility?

5. Is there a budget?

6. Does the prospect understand their risk of not making a purchase?

7. What results, specifically, does the prospect hope to achieve, and what will happen if they do nothing?

8. Does the prospect understand the money/solution ratio—
   what it costs if they do nothing, and how much they save
   if they make a purchase?

We know now that knowing the answers to these questions
won't get us a closed sale, and what a small portion of the sale we've
been addressing.

Listening for systems with my unbiased ear, I can recognize a
buyer's ability to change, and the probability of them being in a position to purchase my product, in the first moments of a prospecting
call. However, sometimes it may not be obvious: Even if they don't
seem ready to buy, or are unaware of what excellence might look
like (I can facilitate possibilities where none existed), I can lead
them down a route of change if they have the right systems elements in place. Then, I teach them on the first call how to have the
Buying Decision Team present on our next meeting. They need to
get all of the appropriate people on board, and I am helping them do
it sooner.

> If their system is not
> capable of change,
> they are not prospects.

I only spend time with those
who are good prospects; I walk
away from folks I can tell will
never buy.

Note: It's important to avoid
falling into the trap of assuming
that if prospects have a need
and money that they would be buyers. If their system is not capable
of change, they are not prospects.

Here is what we'll hear with prospects who will *never* buy:

- They believe they are doing really well and getting such
  excellent results that they wouldn't even consider adding
  anything new.

A bit of caution here: Often sellers are so pushy on the phone
that prospects will say that all is great, and nope, nothing is needed.

I begin the conversation using Buying Facilitation® from the very start of the call, to show the prospect that I'm there to serve. I might say something like:

Sounds like your folks are doing an excellent job. How will you know when it's time to add new skills to what you're already doing so well?

■ The ego of the prospect is such that nothing new could enter without making him/her seem inadequate. Don't assume because you can recognize a real need that the prospect is a buyer. You'll hear things like:

No. We do this ourselves. Always have. Never brought in anyone to do it for us. And we're happy with our results.

Again, use caution here. This might be a response to defending against you being pushy. Using Facilitating Questions might help the person open up possibilities.

■ The prospect really doesn't see a need, and truly is happy— even with their current solution provider. After all, you'd want your prospects to defend you as well.

When you hear any of the above, you probably do not have a buyer. Leave them with the following, in case they want a future resource:

What would you need to know about us to know we'd be able to offer you solutions/skills for those times in the future when your situation changes?

That way, they will ask for your number, or suggest a call back in six months, and remember you as being respectful and supportive, rather than pushy and obnoxious.

TEN STEPS TO MAKING DECISIONS

Here are the steps buyers take as they begin considering solving a problem. Remember: We will not be uncovering need, finding out who the decision makers are or discussing our solution: that will happen later in the conversation.

Note: Depending on the size of the sale, the steps below may or may not be taken at separate times. Sometimes it's possible to lead the buyer through all of the steps on the first call. Sometimes it takes a number of calls. But the buyer must address each of these steps regardless of the time factor.

10 Buying Steps

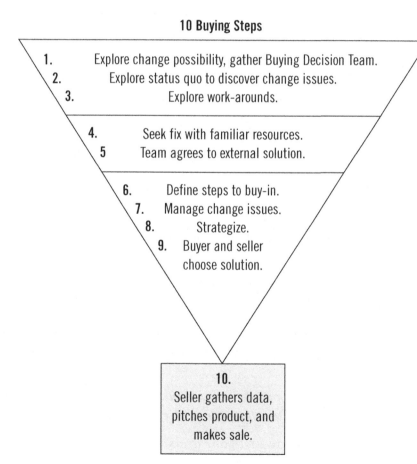

1. Explore change possibility, gather Buying Decision Team.
2. Explore status quo to discover change issues.
3. Explore work-arounds.

4. Seek fix with familiar resources.
5. Team agrees to external solution.

6. Define steps to buy-in.
7. Manage change issues.
8. Strategize.
9. Buyer and seller choose solution.

10.
Seller gathers data, pitches product, and makes sale.

Step 1

Have Initial Contact. Buyer discovers if they are willing and able to consider move toward excellence. *Initial discussions to be introduced to Identified Problem with an exploration of a commitment to pursue change.*

The first call is devoted to helping buyers discover the distance between where they are and excellence, and teaching them how to start the internal conversation needed for change to be considered. We help the buyer recognize what sort of buy-in issues will crop up and how to start navigating the change issues.

As sellers we know what 'excellence' looks like. We know what a dysfunctional environment looks like. Listen through that filter.

By the end of this first contact, the prospect will recognize who should be on the Buying Decision Team and commit to gather them together to meet with you. I understand this doesn't happen using the typical sales model. But using Buying Facilitation® and directing the conversation to the necessary off-line buy-in issues, the stakeholders need to be involved to discover solutions for themselves. Buyer reaction to this process is extremely different, as we are all on the same page: Helping the buyer manage their systems issues en route to excellence.

With our help the buyer will begin to recognize their Identified Problem as a piece of something larger.

We can do this on cold calls, prospecting calls, telemarketing calls, and affect the chance of a purchase right from the beginning.

During the journey down the buyer's change management issues, follow the sequence of the decision phases with your Facilitative Questions:

How will you and your decision team know when it's time to add some new X to what you're already doing?

What has stopped you and your decision team from using the internal group to resolve this?

Facilitative Questions lead buyers through their systems issues to recognize the sorts of decisions they must make. We are actually teaching our buyers how to buy.

Step 2

Explore Status Quo. Focus on willingness to change and work together. *Buying team explores the routes to change and collaboration, the historic issues that led to the Identified Problem. Plan future dates for internal meetings between decision groups. Research begins.*

Here the prospects explore the rules, relationships, and initiatives that hold the Identified Problem in place, and begin to discover the sorts of issues they will have to manage. They must agree to work together and share responsibilities. This speeds up their decision cycle dramatically. With our help, buyers can efficiently begin this early discovery, and we are on the Buying Decision Team.

Until or unless the prospects all agree that it's time to make a change and that they cannot get where they want to be from where they are, they will do nothing. Facilitate their discovery.

Step 3

Explore Work-Arounds. Decision team discovers work-arounds that manage the Identified Problem. *Examines elements of work-arounds and identifies any problems that would result from change. Decide if change is an option and how they should move forward if a new solution is preferable.*

We don't know what this step looks like until it happens, and can only follow it to the extent that we're allowed to. But we must continue to facilitate all of the activities through our Facilitative Questions, helping them decide if making a change/bringing in a solution is something they want to do now. They must do this with us or without us.

Step 4

Fix with Familiar Resources. Decision team seeks known solution. *Group determines if current vendors or internal resources viable.*

Buyers will do nothing different if they can use what they've got and will go to great lengths to continue using a familiar solution: The internal tech team instead of an external design team; an old vendor or product instead of something new.

Keep directing the buyer to use their familiar resources. They are going to do this anyway, and until they recognize the workaround as incomplete, or if they cannot make a familiar solution work, they will take no further action.

And stay focused on managing the buying decision. It is still not time to discover needs or place product.

Facilitative Questions to use here:

What is stopping your current vendor/your inhouse group from managing this problem for you?

If familiar resources are inappropriate, buyer and seller can strategize about how to get the full set of appropriate folks onto the Buying Decision Team. By now, the need has been determined. What is missing is how—or if—to fix it.

Step 5

Agree on External Fix. Decision team agrees to seek an external solution but must maintain systems integrity. *The decision team determines how current work-arounds would meld with a new solution and assesses possible fallout.*

Here is where the heavy-duty tactical work begins. The team must discuss possible options to change, budgets, personnel, and roadblocks. Then, and only then, do they consider if a new purchase is viable. If the answer is 'yes', buyer and seller begin to strategize. Buying Facilitation® actually helps people get on board here, and highlights the upcoming or potential problems that should be monitored. Sellers understand this from past experience.

This is the time you get tactical and help buyers discover how to prepare for a change:

- What teams would need to work together?

- What old initiatives need to be revisited?

- What other departments must get involved?

- What vendors must be considered?

- What HR functions need to be managed?

Remember that they must manage the tangle of issues that touch the Identified Problem. Our solution data are merely one aspect of the range of issues they must consider.

This is often the time when people start seeking data, doing Sales 2.0 activities, reading books, calling colleagues, etc. We can offer them general information about our product or service, but they are still not close to a buying decision.

Step 6

Define Steps to Buy-In. Buyer/seller strategizing around change. *The team decides who else to add to decision team to ensure total buy-in to move forward, and searches for what else needs to be addressed in order to avoid systems disruption.*

The larger the sale, the larger the group of stakeholders and decision partners, the longer this part of the facilitation cycle will last. This step usually constitutes half of the sales cycle. There are no clear decisions yet and your decision facilitation will save huge amounts of time.

Help them make sure they have included all of the stakeholders and make sure they understand all possibilities for fallout. No sale will happen until all of this is complete.

Step 7

Manage Internal Change Issues. Stakeholder buy-in throughout the system. *Stakeholders to take responsibility for change: to move forward according to the needs of the systems components; to discover problem areas; to note where the status quo would face disruption; to find funds and plan timing.*

We've never been able to influence these activities before. Now we're on the Buying Decision Team and can lead the buyers through their decisions. It's very tricky: We have no long-term political capital with the Buying Decision Team, and are limited by our outsider status. It's a good idea to send the buyer lists of Facilitative Questions that will prove helpful and also keep the seller on the buyer's decision team. It's imperative to stay away from any sort of pitch.

Step 8

Take Action. Decision team strategizes to take action. *Buyer and seller discuss money, time, personnel, change management, implementation issues, and buy-in issues.*

It's amazing how easy this step is. And since the buyer has already decided, there are no price objections. Price objections happen when buyers don't understand the full value proposition in relation to their change issues. Once they understand, price isn't an issue.

I recently had a client who was suffering in the economy and asked me if I could drop my price. I told him I certainly could do that, but would have to subtract the commensurate service. He said he understood, and then went back to the original price.

By now, the prospect knows:

■ They are ready to change and add something new.

■ They cannot handle the change by using their existing resources.

■ What they need to do to move forward and ensure systems congruency.

■ The players that must be involved.

■ How to go about getting buy-in.

Step 9

Move Forward. Buyer and Seller manage internal change. *Final discussions of logistics, and the repetition of any of above steps.*

Help the decision team go through all elements of how a solution will be used, how the decision team needs to manage problems or work-arounds, what risks remain exposed for the system, and whatever issues remain unresolved.

Step 10

Sell. Seller gathers data, presents product, makes pitch. *Solution specifications are presented in relation to the buying patterns and decision criteria.*

It's time to do your sales job: gather specifics about the outcomes that a new solution will offer; understand the full range of needs; understand and offer thoughts about the people who will use your solution; offer details about your solution in terms of the buying criteria that the buyer just discovered.

Before now we've typically pitched into a void with no understanding of what is being listened to, or what the prospect is doing with that information. Because we've facilitated their decision to change, the prospect will already know who, why, what, when, and how they need to buy, so your pitch will be an information exchange, rather than an influencing strategy.

BUYING DECISIONS AND PRICE

These ten phases comprise the string of events that buyers need to complete. Now, by facilitating their route through their system and decision making, we've taught them how to manage their own change issues and be ready to choose a solution.

We've never been a part of this end of the path of change before. Now we can make their process far more efficient. It's frustrating because we can't do it *for* them, but we can do it *with* them, and provide the route. It will accelerate their process for them, and make them so much more efficient.

It's vital that we don't use these stages as an opportunity to push our product. If you hear any objections at all along the way, you most likely have pushed your solution before they have made their necessary internal decisions.

When you facilitate decisions instead of focusing on placing solutions, objections are impossible: The model merely helps the prospect make decisions and manage change without demanding they buy anything.

One January 11, I got a call from a sales manager interested in hiring me to do training with his group. As I led him down his steps, I used this question:

What has stopped you from having the level of success you're now seeking?

His response: *Let me call you back.*

On Dec. 17 of that same year, Jack called me back.

You know that question you asked me last year? Well, I put it up on my desk, knowing that I needed an answer to it. Kicking and screaming, I had to admit that I was what was stopping us. My beliefs, my staffing choices, my rules.

Over the past year, I've made the changes we need to make to get onto the route toward success. Now we're ready for you. Send me your contract and let me know your first available dates.

I got off the phone and began putting together a contract. But there was one issue we forgot to discuss. I called back:

Hey, Jack. We never discussed price and I want to let you know what's going to be on the contract.

He replied:

What difference does it make? You've already paid for yourself.

Once we are on the decision team, and help the buyer design a solution that involves all of the systems issues, it's not about our price. It's only when buyers can't differentiate between two things does price become an issue. You will have proven yourself to be an asset and already be on their team: Price will not be a big discussion.

A NOTE OF EXPLANATION

Initially, you might find it confusing to lead a prospect through their decision making without understanding their 'need' and not be discussing your solution.

Once you thoroughly understand systems, and how decisions get made, and how 'need' sits in a system, you'll quickly be able to hear what the buyer has to contend with. Because purchasing a solution, getting the right decision makers on board, and managing the commensurate change are unfamiliar tasks, you'll have far greater skills than the buyer. Remember: You are being a leader here—not a seller.

Trust that your experience in your field will help you lead prospects through their stages. Just stay out of product pitch, stay away from trying to understand needs, and listen with your 'systems listening' ear: Hear where they need decision made, listen for systems problems they may have while considering adding a new solution, and help them make sure they can't resolve the problem themselves.

It's a new job. It's that part of the buying decision process we've never been a part of before now.

Once you're a proven Leader and Change Agent, you will be the chosen solution provider, regardless of price.

Let's take a look at Sales 2.0 in the next chapter, and then put everything we learned together, in Section Three.

SALES 2.0:
THE BLESSING AND THE CURSE

"In 1876, Alexander Graham Bell's invention of the telephone provided the first technological alternative to information exchange by mail or in person. In more recent times, we have access to a dazzling array of online products, mobile devices, and automated services that are changing the way we communicate, and therefore, how customers buy and how sellers sell. However, despite more than a century of technological advancement, we still have sales productivity challenges."

—Preface of *Sales 2.0* by Anneke Seley and Brent Holloway.

In Chapter 11, we'll examine Sales 2.0, and see what it means to our jobs.

During the chapter:

■ We will see how Sales 2.0 resembles the sales system we're familiar with;

■ We will ask some questions about how to succeed in the Sales 2.0 environment.

TECHNOLOGY certainly makes the sales portion of our jobs easier. But take care: Sales 2.0 is merely an extension of the conventional sales model, continuing the same systemic thinking via the use of technology, but with

- more capability to connect with prospects than ever before,

- more ways to offer the right product info to the right person,

- more ways to collect data of interested strangers,

- more ways to offer great service,

- more capability of offering a way to understand and be understood,

- more ways to drive traffic to our sites,

- the assumption that data for need resolution is the primary reason buyers seek answers on the web.

We have websites, email marketing, webinars, podcasts, blogs, Twitter and LinkedIn, Fast Pitch and RSS. We can measure if our brand name is getting the attention we seek, and who is finding us.

We can offer free lead generating material so buyers can learn about us, while we track and measure their responses. We can receive contact from—and sell products to—strangers we hadn't known were interested in our products.

Indeed, even if I listed all of the capability that now exists on the web to help us sell and help our buyers buy, it would be out of date by the end of the week. So much wonderful and exciting change.

And yet, what exactly is it changing? As it says in the last line of the opening quote, "….we still have sales productivity challenges."

MANAGING THE SALE, NOT THE BUYING DECISION

Sales 2.0 seems to be brilliant. Yes, it can find and track new customers, find data and products that used to take huge marketing campaigns, and give us information so we can change on a dime to ensure the best messaging and pricing. There is even a company called SalesGenuis that is set up to make immediate—that's 'immediate'- contact with someone who fills out a form, or clicks on a site!

But what does this change? And what does this assume?

The assumptions remain the same: that a prospect who shows interest in data about your offering is ready, willing, and able to buy. By now we know that's a faulty assumption.

Sales 2.0

- makes product/solution data ubiquitous so the person 'ready to buy' can get targeted data,

- allows sellers to increase their prospect data base,

- drives prospects to sites of potential solution providers,

- exhibits product data,

- makes many types of information available instantly,

- starts a conversation,

- offers purchasing capability.

But it does *not* help manage the subjective, values-based criteria of the buying decision. It does *not* help the buyer's meetings get set up quicker. It does *not* help the person in the next department, or the next room, agree to do something different. So the productivity challenges will continue.

Sales 2.0 also doesn't manage the true essence of collaboration.

How does one person connect with another in a way that both are served authentically?

How can technology help drive the full set of buying decisions buyers need to consider?

I suspect the second question is answerable; the first isn't. But let's keep both on the table.

SALES 2.0 DRIVES PURCHASE AS LAST DECISION

I'm going to admit here that I don't have a complete answer to how Sales 2.0 can drive a buying decision. But I have a lot of questions.

Let me begin by summarizing the obvious: The on-line capability is product/solution/information based. We share information, measure input, tag prospects, and elicit data to track buying behaviors to learn how to eventually drive buyers into our databases so we can contact them personally, and sell a product.

Using the internet as the means to attempt to pull in business, we continue to limit our job description to that of 'solution consultant' rather than 'decision facilitator.' Just because buyers can educate themselves, and sellers can track, test, and measure what the buyer is doing, doesn't mean off-line buying decisions are going to be made.

Here are the faulty assumptions I see built in here:

1. If buyers are seeking data from us, they are ready, willing and able to buy.

2. If buyers take a webinar, or read a blog, or copy a free white paper, they are at least hot prospects.

3. The power of the sale moves from seller to buyer.

4. If buyers read or use some of our information or view our site, they are open to making a purchase.

Sellers actually believe those assumptions. A close friend of mine who is a well-known best-selling author of sales books keeps saying to me, "It's all about the database. You want to keep collecting names. Give away free stuff so you can get more names. It's all about the database." And my response is: "What will you do with it?"

Recently I've heard the number '20% close rate' thrown around by savvy folks in the Sales 2.0 field: that companies using Sales 2.0 close 20% of prospects. What does that number mean? Twenty percent of people who search the site? Get followed? Get call backs? Go to free webinars? Make contact personally? And where are the other 80% going?

WHEN DO BUYERS MAKE A PURCHASE?

Who is helping them decide how to take action?

Acting as if it's a numbers game, sending out X emails will obviously give you Y % success. Is this what it's about? Are we not just doing what we've always done, only faster, with a broader reach, and targeted with more specificity?

Don't the same problems with buyers buying arise but are mitigated because we're playing with higher numbers of prospects?

Obviously, with more contact, greater numbers of prospects, the ability for ads to be tested before being rolled out, and more ability for buyers who are ready to buy to find the exact data they need when they need it, the probability exists to close more. This is a suped-up numbers game.

Coupled with the ability to discover a highly targeted demographic through cookies and social networking sites, Sales 2.0 will close more sales because of sheer numbers. Not to mention those prospects who needed only data to complete their decision making are going to have the means to find the right solution much easier.

> Until buyers are ready, willing, and able to buy, and their systems are lined up and ready to make a change and a purchase, they will not buy.

I believe that we experience the exact same issues with Sales 2.0 as we do with sales. Until buyers are ready, willing, and able to buy, and their systems are lined up and ready to make a change and a purchase, they will not buy.

And the only people who will buy are those who are already ready, whose systems have given agreement and all they need is your product information.

In *Sales 2.0*, (page 147) Seley and Holloway quote Bill Stinnett's book *Think Like Your Customer* (McGraw Hill 2004), saying that Sinnett's six questions that customers must answer before they buy (questions below) are '...an integral part' in the 2.0 environment:

1. What is the customer's business motive and real reason for buying?

2. What is the urgency? What is the impending event?

3. What is the impact, payback, or results they expect to receive?

4. What are the consequences of doing nothing?

5. What resources or means are available?

6. What is the risk associated with making a decision?

If you've read this far in the book, you'll know that the above questions are specious: *Sellers can't know the answers to these questions on behalf of the buyer!*

If they had a guess as to the answer, they wouldn't have valid data because the buyer probably doesn't know the answers initially, and when they do, they will know exactly what they are ready to buy.

Sales 2.0 can then respond immediately. But not until then. So in effect, we're still focusing on the solution decision end of the sales cycle, and have not managed the buying decision end. But I think it's possible to add that.

QUESTIONS TO ASK OURSELVES TO HAVE MORE SUCCESS

I'm going to pose some questions and reservations I have about Sales 2.0, and simultaneously add some decision facilitation sugges-tions so you can influence the top of the buying decision funnel as well as the bottom.

Question: How can we get someone who signs up for a webinar to buy something?

Guess: People come to webinars either out of general curiosity or because they have some interest in making a change and adding some new capability.

The only way I can think of helping them make a purchase would be to use Facilitative Questions. Should I put the Facilitative Questions in a questionnaire before the webinar? That would help them know what to do with the webinar data because they would then know where the data would fit. But then what? I still have to wait for them to call me. Or should I call them with more Facilitative Questions?

Just because they fill out a questionnaire doesn't mean they want a call from me or that they are ready to buy. It's still a one-way communication. Unless I use their contact data to place a call and walk them through the Buying Facilitation® process. SalesGenius does just this. Do you want to do that?

Question: How do we convert a site visitor to an active prospect?

Guess: How can we predict a prospect's buying patterns?
I could probably develop a software program that leads site

visitors down their implicit buying decision process so we could predict the prospect's buying patterns and lead them to a decision. But how would I get them to answer these questions? And who would answer? Probably those people ready to buy anyway.

I know that several books suggest that we use a telemarketing group to make contact with folks who have opted-in and given us permission (in one way or another) to contact them. But just because we have their names or because they've heard our webinar, doesn't mean they are active.

Of course, Buying Facilitation® would help, but we would certainly need an agreement from them to use their phone number, or get permission by sending an email request. In either case, assuming they might buy our product is not automatic just because they have visited our site or taken a webinar.

Question: How do you know that the criteria you choose as a 'pipeline' are indeed the steps for any particular buying decision, whether it's Sales 2.0 or typical sales?

Guess: Sure—we've arbitrarily chosen steps to highlight the route that a 'high potential' prospect would follow en route to a buying decision. We've had that sort of pipeline for years.

Just because a prospect has money, or a need, or seems to be actively looking for a solution, doesn't mean they are buyers. We've seen that in this book over and over. That's why we have a 90% failure rate: We've assumed this is true.

USING BUYING FACILITATION® WITH SALES 2.0

Given that Sales 2.0 is here to stay, I'm going to make a few suggestions as to how to drive a buying decision from the technology. As you read the rest of the chapter, think of ways to faciliate decisions.

1. Increase your exposure: do webinars, podcasts, blogs, and comment on other people's blogs and in groups such as LinkedIn. This will help you reach those people who have a possible Identified Problem in the area that your marketing functions. Marketing campaigns are so much easier these days, with data mining, and instant feedback as to whether a campaign is successful or not. So make sure sales and marketing are working closely together.

2. In your outreach, pose Facilitative Questions to lead folks through their buying decisions. I've developed a front-end decision tool (HOBBES®) that does this. You can create your own. Just remember to lead them through their own answers, rather than directing them to your products.

3. Find ways to encourage curiosity about the implicit buying decision vs. the explicit one. One of my favorite questions to do this is:

   What is stopping you from closing all of the sales you should be closing?

4. Find a method to drive some sort of 'demand generation' interaction that gives you the ability to connect directly, via an inbound group, so you can facilitate the decisions. It's possible to create technology, or a phone sales campaign, that will lead the buyer through all of their decision criteria—but without finding some way of managing this issue, your closed sales will continue to be a fraction of what they should be.

Use Sales 2.0 as a piece of the sales model. Just remember that until or unless the buyer makes a purchasing decision, it doesn't matter what you've got or what you're doing.

In the final section of the book, we're going to go through a Case Study of a sale from every angle. I'll also illustrate the skills of facilitating the decision. Enjoy.

THE SKILLS: PUTTING IT ALL TOGETHER

"The corporation is becoming naked. Corporations have no choice but to rethink their values and behavior—to integrate corporate citizenship into their DNA. If you're going to be naked, you'd better be buff!

As a result, customer centricity is being turned upside down. Rather than simply listening to customers, companies must and can truly engage them. Customers have become value creators themselves through new forms of collaboration....The brand, rather than being just an image, promise, or 'word in the mind' as it's called, can become, in part, an actual relationship between a company and its customers."

—**Don Tapscott,** foreward to Denise Shiffman's book *The Age of Engage: Reinventing Marketing for Today's Connected, Collaborative, and Hyperinteractive Culture.*

CASE STUDY:
ANATOMY OF A BUYING DECISION

Chapter 12 is a replica of a typical sale. The scenario will follow a buyer through his discovery and management of every element he needs to address during a typical buying decision. Note the time elements, people and relationship issues, company politics, and the decision criteria.

During the chapter:

- We will sit by the side of the buyer as he works his way through his company issues, tries to garner buy-in from colleagues, and chooses a vendor;

- We will discuss the buying decision issues and the vendor's selling issues.

IT'S TIME TO PUT all of the pieces together with an important reminder: a buyer needs to resolve a problem. Period. They don't want our offering. They don't want a good price. They don't want a nice vendor. They only want to resolve their problem in a way that's congruent with their system.

We also know that if they can use an internal, or familiar, solution, they'd prefer it, and that before they make a purchase they must get buy-in from all elements that touch the Identified Problem.

We know the rules of systems and how they affect the culture buyers live in, how the shifts going on in the world are changing our business climate because the system is shifting with the economic influences.

It's time to add the decision facilitation tools into the mix. We've got the background; now let's do it.

THE SET UP OF THE SKILLS SECTION

Over the next three chapters, we're going to be entering a buyer's environment and walking with him through each stage of his buying decision process. We're also going to follow a vendor through her sales process.

To ensure accuracy, I called several friends who know the anatomy of a sale in the web-design/technology category. We broke down every activity that a buyer must go through in a typical corporate situation including how and when the decision makers were folded in, and how and when the vendors were brought in.

We then figured out the amount of time each aspect, each meeting, each decision took. They came up with 44 weeks; it sounded too high to me so I downsized it to 36 weeks. I later spoke with a seller in the exact same situation and he told me that he was still waiting for the final agreement after 13 months: He'd been to see the prospect three times, he'd had many calls to follow up, and he was recently told they were 90% ready to go but still needed 'some time.'

Enjoy the section. It will open your eyes to why we face the frustrations we face every day as a vendor, and have some compassion for what our buyers are going through on their end. And, ultimately, we'll learn a new way to sell that not only closes more sales, but also makes it possible to serve our buyers.

WHO IS THE BUYER SUPPORT PERSON?

To let you know how ingrained the sales model is, I want to share a story of what happens when I teach sales folks to think about the buy-in necessary for a purchase to happen.

In my company, we run a two-day Facilitating Buying Decisions program to teach sellers how to understand every aspect of a buying decision. In one of the exercises, there are three roles: Seller, Buyer, and a Buyer Support person. No one sees each other's instruction card, of course. The Buyer Support card which represents the unseen systems elements that 'control' the buyer's buying decision, specifically explains the reasons why this person won't allow the Buyer to work with a different vendor, spend money, etc. In other words, this person is the 'Nay Sayer.'

During this exercise, each person gets to play all three roles, so they understand the buying decision from each aspect: Of course they are familiar with being a seller, having had years of experience with buyers, but they (similar to many sales folks) are not familiar with the important function that the people in the buyer's environment play in the buying decision. Hence the reason for the exercise.

During the exercise, time after time, I watch while the person playing the Seller ignores the person playing the Buyer Support role, *even after they have played that role, read their role card, and understand that the sale can't happen without a new decision from this person.*

The person playing the Seller absolutely cannot seem to get off pitch, or relationship building. This seller cannot even address—for a moment!—the person sitting right next to the Buyer! Even though the person is the real decision maker! And they don't understand why someone who is not "The Buyer" has any influence and should be included in the discussion. In the post-exercise Q&A they look at me in confusion. "Why did you throw that Buyer Support card in there? What were we supposed to do with that?"

One time, the Seller role was played by a line salesperson, and her manager played the Buyer Support role. In that role play, the Buyer Support person scenario was a majority shareholder with an active role in signing off on expenditures; the Buyer was a visionary who loved finding new things to buy and try. At the time of the role play situation, the Buyer had been on a spending spree; the Buyer Support role was to stop the Buyer from spending any more money.

During the role play, the Seller totally ignored the Buyer Support person, preferring instead to develop a delightful relationship with the Buyer. And boy, was the Buyer pumped. They *loved* each other, made promises, talked implementation, and so on.

After the role play, the flushed Seller turned to her boss—whom she had ignored for 30 minutes—and said, "Closed it."

"No you didn't."

"Of course I did," she said.

"No you didn't. I'm not allowing him to spend any money."

"You're wrong," she said. "I nailed it."

The manager showed her his card, pointing out that the top decision maker would never allow any expenditure. She read the card, thought about it for a moment, and then said, "I don't care what this card says. I nailed it, and it's a closed sale."

So much for reality.

THE SCENARIO

Here is the set up for the sales situation we'll be playing with in the next four chapters. I made it as real as possible, and this set of events and timing were approved by three different sales folks. Enjoy.

THE BUYER'S STORY

Scenario

Background: Joe Sternblatt is a marketing manager of a 150-person manufacturing company. He joined the company about eight months ago and is quite happy there. He's effected change, had some success, and believes it's now time to begin to fully integrate the internet, social marketing, and a good, solid web design into the company brand.

His initial obvious problem is that he hasn't had much of a relationship with the sales department. While they have made a few tentative stabs at connecting—one rather cordial lunch initiated by Joe—they share no vision or strategic initiatives.

The company really doesn't foster collaboration—everyone seems to work as if an island. The branding and customer service managers have issues, with customer service sometimes at odds with the branding manager's initiatives, and certainly always in some sort of tiff with sales. The branding team works by itself, believing that they are better than the rest. And the company has had no initiative or agenda around getting the groups to work together.

Until now the internal tech team has designed and managed the company website. It hasn't been particularly creative and doesn't use a lot of the more modern technology, like social networking, or customer surveys. But it has done the job of offering company data. Their web views have been mid-range—'acceptable.'

Identified Problem: Joe wants a more professional and interactive web site. He is not happy with recent studies that show that their site isn't getting the traffic they should be getting. Nor are they using their web presence in the most proactive manner: the site should be so much more than a brochure. But the tech guys have so much other work to do and they aren't savvy designers.

Joe thinks it's time for a professional web design group to come in and take over from the in-house tech team. He doesn't believe that the internal group has the skills to design an up-to-date site that will both create a client community and get the marketing department (Joe's group) the data they need. Plus, he wants to use some Sales 2.0 methods to drive traffic to the site, have a group of rotating bloggers, have some marketing offers of free stuff, and possibly have the sales team do some calls to folks who send in the Contact forms.

Joe is willing to take on the challenge of finding a good design group, as well as doing the work of getting the obvious departments to work together. He understands he has an uphill battle getting people to agree.

Joe knows he runs the risk of not being seen as a team player. Until now he's gone along with the rest. And he knows they have political capital he doesn't have. But he believes that it's so important now, with this economy, with this much change going on, to have a website that does what it is meant to do: Prove that their company is professional and authentic, cares about customers, and is ready to listen to customers as part of their brand. The competition advertises similar products on their site and offers great promotions, podcasts and community building. It's killing Joe's business.

Joe believes they need to do something immediately. To get this to happen, he's got to bring sales, marketing, branding, and customer service together to work more closely.

He'll start developing the relationships. He should have done it months ago anyway. His goal, of course, is to get them to agree to a new web design from an outside group, and get them to help pay for it.

There is currently no budget for a site redesign because all tech work has been done in-house. Given that the tech manager reports directly to the CFO, it's a good bet that the CFO would want her tech folks to do any site work and won't provide budget for someone to do the work her team should be doing.

Joe is hoping that the expense of a new design vendor could be shared with the partner teams, taken out of line items or travel. But first they'll need to agree to do the site redesign.

Joe is ultimately going to have to figure out a way to get buy-in from the CFO. She hasn't shown any particular penchant for creativity or for using the web for promotions or customer outreach.

No one in the company is even doing a blog. Joe will have to get her up to speed and show her some numbers—how much business they are losing to the competition—so she'll understand the importance of beefing up the website.

Hidden systems elements:

1. *Work-around:* Current tech team has been doing site designs and maintenance ever since they put up a website, as part of their normal responsibilities. There is no dedicated group, but all tech team members enjoy doing parts of the web work as well as the other programming needed by the departments. A new tech manager started six months ago and all managers like him a lot.

2. *Management collaboration:* Current teams have very little interaction, although it would seem obvious that sales, marketing, branding, and customer service should be working closely together. But the culture has no political capital around collaboration. In fact, the managers are quite competitive for funds, and hostile with each other, never sharing ideas or projects. As a result, sometimes there is overlap on initiatives and funding.

3. *Budget:* There is no budget for this site redesign. Money would have to come from partner teams (who have never shared budget before), or the CFO (who has no criteria around changing the site design).

4. *External vendors:* No external vendors have been used for tech stuff; all technical work has been done in house.

Joe has plotted out a route through the problem that involves getting into partnership with his colleagues, then getting buy-in for a site redesign so he can get their help, input, and funds, and then getting the group to influence the CFO to give them money or approval.

They will use prospective vendors to give them the details of what they might do, and have the tech team compete for the business. And then choose one of the vendors. Hopefully, they will get the approval to move forward and do the design and the implementation without the internal tech team being involved in any way. Fingers crossed.

THE SALES CYCLE

Chain of Events

1. Meet/Create the Buying Decision Team. Joe starts having informal lunch meetings with each of the other collegial managers: the sales manger, brand manager,   and customer services manager. He focuses on starting collaborative relationships.

It's not going well with the sales manager, but there is some opening with the others. Joe starts conversations about their thoughts on the current web design. He discusses the site traffic, shows the report that has the company lagging in the competition, and starts a discussion around possibilities for a more professional web site. He tries to get agreement.

Joe discusses doing some research on different sorts of sites, different outcomes of social networking, podcasting, and customer outreach via Sales 2.0 He also brings up the differences between hiring an external web team vs. using their current team and the problems inherent in each.

During several informal lunches, he discusses technology choices, possible vendors, SEO, and so on. Although they don't start planning, at least the discussions have begun. He gets mixed responses about keeping the project in-house versus bringing in a professional web design team. And, the sales manager continues to be somewhat hostile to any ideas other than her own. Other colleagues finally agree to research web design options.

(Time elapsed: 3 weeks)

2. Hold Group Meeting with Colleagues. The managers meet. Joe chooses not to discuss some of his research, or get the tech folks and CFO involved until the group joins forces and decides what they want to do. Hopefully he can convince them to see it his way.

He gets them to discuss who would have interest in a new website. Do they want the tech work to remain in-house or can they consider an outside vendor? Managers are not so happy with tech team, but they want to give the new tech manager the chance to shape up. They don't hold out much hope given what they've seen to date, but think he deserves a chance.

They each agree to think about choices and come up with some thoughts and ideas about needs and possibilities. They agree to have Joe have an information-gathering meeting with the tech manager. Joe decides to not mention the fact that they have never worked together as a 'team' and figures that as this progresses, they will realize how much they need each other.

(Time elapsed: 2 weeks)

3. Meet with Tech Manager. Joe meets with the tech manager to discuss discontent about the current site design and the competitive report showing how much business they are losing. Joe wants to hear his thoughts on the current site, and learn about future plans.

He asks him to begin thinking about site redesign and shares that he'll be doing research as well about upgrading their site design and capability. Joe tells the tech manager that the other managers have interest in a possible redesign also.

(Time elapsed: 1 week)

4. Meet Vendors. Joe invites four vendors to present their capability so Joe understands what's possible—how the new bells and whistles of web sites could benefit them. What could it look like for their company? How would it look in relation to the competition? How could it drive business? How could they compete? How would Sales 2.0 be instituted? What would it demand from each of the groups?

(Time elapsed: 2 weeks)

5. Meet with Colleagues. Joe meets with sales, customer service, and brand managers. He listens to the ideas they researched, and shares data gleaned from vendors. Topic for discussion: Can our in-house team give us anything close to what a new vendor could offer? How will we know? Brainstorm.

Team agrees to have Joe meet with CFO to discuss possibilities and need for more professional website. The group discusses next steps and how to handle tech team. They agree to sit down with the tech team once Joe brings back the issues raised by the CFO if it becomes clear that she is not inclined to want to do anything new. Joe asks to be Project Manager of the site redesign.

The sales manager is having a hard time staying with the project. She's got her own external PR group that creates a campaign with each new product launch, and she's been meeting her numbers every year. Joe must have one more lunch with her to find a way to get aligned.

(Time elapsed: 3 weeks)

6. Meet with CFO. Joe presents data from competitive web sites to the CFO. He outlines the current needs of the brand, sales, marketing, and customer service managers. He discusses how a new site design could enhance the company's market position, bring in new business, and give customers a vehicle to communicate. Joe shows her some competitor's web sites. He explains the offerings from the vendors, and the discussions with the tech group.

The CFO doesn't have any particular interest in doing a web-redesign. But if Joe and the rest of the teams push, she'd want it to remain in-house unless they prove to her there would be a difference in results. She states that there is no budget and thinks the idea is a waste of time and money given that the company is meeting their numbers and doing well financially. She tells them that they would have to find the funds from their own budgets if they are adamant about going outside for a vendor.

Joe must get some numbers together to prove it would be cost effective to use an outsider provider. And show her that her numbers are deflated—they should be bringing in more business, but aren't because of the web tactics competitors are using.

(Time elapsed: 2 weeks)

7. Meet Again with Tech Team. Joe brings ideas gleaned from the vendor presentations to the tech group and discusses some ideas he has put together for a new site.

He asks how long it would take to come up with a redesign, and do the research, design, test, and implementation. He asks the tech manager to start thinking about all of the possibilities. They set up a time to sit down and gather specs. He also gets agreement to meet with the vendor groups to see if their presentations will give the tech guy any ideas on what he needs to do.

(Time elapsed: 1 week)

8. Tech Team Meets with Managers and Vendors. Vendors come in again to present to the Buying Decision Team. All managers and tech manager are included. They discuss costs and timing and the possibility of the vendor doing the site design while collaborating with the tech group for programming. They all discuss possibilities of vendors doing the entire project, with no help from the internal team. They discuss the tech team doing the entire project with no outside help. They discuss time frames. The managers ask questions, vet ideas, offer suggestions.

Following the meeting, Joe asks the tech manager to put together a new presentation, and offer thoughts on collaborating with a vendor versus doing it all in house. The tech manager is not happy.

The tech manager tells everyone he'll contact them to gather the data he needs to put together a presentation for them. His plan is to create something better than the vendors presented.

(Time elapsed: 2 weeks)

9. Meet with Managers. The managers get together to collaborate and brainstorm to decide if they want to use their in-house group or an external group. They must also discuss time frames and budgets, and figure out where to get funds if the CFO won't release money. Would they have available funds in their budgets? They must put together a report to give to the CFO once they decide what they want and who they want to use. They all agree to meet with the CFO.

Joe can tell there is a problem brewing. The managers are jockeying for position, the sales teams are saying they don't need to participate since they have their own vendor, the customer service group saying that sales should pay for the whole thing, and everyone is holding their cards close to the chest.

(Time elapsed: 2 weeks)

10. Meet with Managers and the Tech Team. Joe and the other managers meet with the tech team to see their ideas for the site design. All of the managers bring and discuss their individual specs.

They discuss the possibility of the tech group working alongside a vendor in case the team decides to have the vendor do the site design. Would they be willing to collaborate with a vendor?

The tech group wants to do all the work. But if they cannot match the vision and capability of the vendors, or do it in a reasonable time frame, it's not worth it.

(Time elapsed: 2 weeks)

11. Management Team Meeting. The managers meet to decide how to move forward: Should a vendor do the whole job, or just do the design while the internal team does the implementation? How does this get funded if we use a vendor? Who pays what percentages? Who is responsible for what? Who will be responsible for the implementation? Would the tech team get involved if the external vendor does it and the tech guys are hostile? Who gets what space and what capacity? What needs to be accomplished? Problem: Sales is still not on board, but will be a silent partner.

They all get ready to make a presentation to CFO. They divide the responsibilities among the team members.

Joe sets up another lunch meeting with the sales manager to try to convince her to join forces (and budgets).

(Time elapsed: 1 week)

12. Design a Presentation for CFO Presentation. Managers meet several times to develop the presentation for the CFO.

(Time elapsed: 3 weeks)

3. Make Presentation to CFO. The managers make a presentation to the CFO that includes:

   a.   Vendor data, site design choices. Prices. Capabilities at completion.

   b   Choices between having a vendor do the entire project or a vendor doing the site design while the in-house tech team does the implementation and programming. Includes: time elements, financial elements, personnel elements, implementation elements.

   c.   Tech design is presented, along with time frames and costs. Includes projects they will have to put on hold to do this, or alternatively put this site redesign on hold for six months.

d. Managers present a case for financial viability for doing a site redesign with a vendor if the tech team can't complete it in a reasonable time frame.

The CFO will not release any budget and prefers using the internal tech team. She can't understand why vendors would do a better job than the internal team. She also has no feelings of urgency, believing that everyone is going through hard times, and that there are more important things to do with the funds.

When the entire group pushes back, she relents and agrees to have a vendor do the design so long as the managers find their own money. But her main criterion is to have the tech folks be involved as much as possible—certainly to do the programming, regardless of how long it takes.

(Time elapsed: 5 weeks)

14. Final Choices—Meeting with Management Team. Meet with all managers to make some decisions: Are they willing to take funds from their budget? Do they want to see vendors one more time? They decide they'd like to have a vendor group do the site design immediately, and have the tech group do the programming.

They discuss criteria for choosing a vendor. Originally they had wanted the group most technically exciting. Now they have to choose a vendor that knows how to work well with their tech team, knows how to be patient, and knows how to lead without taking over. The CFO will hear about it if there are any slip-ups. They are not sure that they have had the right vendors come in to present, now that the choice criteria have been changed, but they agree to choose the most appropriate from the ones already seen to avoid wasting more time.

A follow-on discussion occurs about which of the four vendors would be most appropriate. Two are chosen using the new criteria.

(Time elapsed: 2 weeks)

15. Data-Gathering Sessions with Vendors; Vendor Presentations. The two favorite vendors come in with final presentations and fees to do just the website design. Following the presentations, the team chooses the vendor that shows the greatest capability of working collaboratively. They were more expensive, but the other vendor never discussed their ability to collaborate—a crucial element in their Identified Problem given the vendor will have to work closely with the tech team.

(Time elapsed: 2 weeks)

16. Financial Discussion. All the team managers must figure out how to contribute funds from their budgets. The sales manager also agrees to contribute, but it was touch-and-go for a few days.

The teams must negotiate how much they should be contributing. There are several internal issues that fall out from group managers concerning who should contribute more/less, who should have more sway with site design, and how their individual groups would be represented on the home page. Indeed, as a result of these negotiations, the sales manager fell out with the other teams, although she reluctantly agreed to give her share of the cost.

Contract developed for vendor.

(Time elapsed: 2 weeks)

17. Meeting with Chosen Vendor and Tech Manager. Figure out how to begin working together.

(Time elapsed: 1 week)

> **Total elapsed time: 36 weeks, mostly spent aligning calendars for meetings, and getting buy-in.**

HOW THE BUYING DECISION AND THE PROJECT PROGRESSED

As Joe continued through the process, the historic issues between the partner teams became more and more problematic—managers who never worked together were cautious, everyone was competitive, and no one wanted to free up money from their budgets. Indeed, except for the tech manager who, surprisingly, really partnered with him, Joe ended up stirring up issues that had troubled him from the time he joined the company, especially the professional clashes with the sales manager who had an historic issue with the marketing department.

Joe spent most of his time having private conversations with each of the managers, getting them to buy in to his vision, only to have the progress delayed once the entire group was together and people were jockeying for position.

Eventually the tech manager told everyone that he realized that one of the vendors was doing some really interesting things with SEO, and Google Adsense, and use of social network marketing. He thought the company would be served best if they chose that vendor.

Ultimately everyone bought into doing a site redesign using a vendor, and having the tech team doing the implementation, programming, and testing. Eventually, they figured out how to divvy up the costs, and meet regularly to jointly decide on site designs and functionality.

SUMMARY OF THE BUYING ENVIRONMENT

As we read this case study with our understanding of systems, decision making, and how an Identified Problem sits within a system, the problems are painfully obvious.

Most of the ultimate needs were unknown when Joe began his search for a solution. Certainly he did not have his full range of criteria for his solution choice. Here is a list of what Joe couldn't know when he started:

1. If the other managers would be willing to collaborate and form a support team;

2. If the other managers would buy in to a tech project and be willing to work together to come up with joint site designs;

3. If the other managers would be willing to seek an outside vendor;

4. If the CFO would have any flexibility or be supportive;

5. If the tech group could come up with a viable site redesign and have time availability to do the work;

6. If the tech group would be willing to work with a vendor to just program the back end of the project;

7. How to choose the vendor and how to get the partner groups to agree on specific criteria for making a choice;

8. If any of the vendors would exhibit collaboration skills. If not, they'd have to go back to the drawing board;

9. How to manage budgetary issues given the history of the partner groups working individually, without partnering;

10. Any technical issues that would be problematic;

11. How the managers— brand, tech, marketing, sales—would work with the new vendor and if there would be any human fallout;

12. How the handover would work between the old and the new groups;

13. How the new and old technology would work together and how to manage any technology issues;

14. If there would be any customer problems with the new site technology;

15. How the customer service people should be involved in case of any problems;

16. How/if to get agreement—and money—from the CFO.

Until or unless these issues were resolved, there would be no sale. Each of the people involved had a series of decisions to make that didn't necessarily involve Joe or the web design problems but factored greatly in the decision to choose a vendor.

The systems issues were pervasive. Obviously any vendor entering into this situation would be a pawn in the corporate drama.

Before we walk over to the seller's side of the table, let's take a look at what would happen if Buying Facilitation® were used from Week 6 when Joe first called the vendors. See how the decision facilitation process helps Joe's decision making process from the first call.

CHAPTER THIRTEEN

HOW BUYING FACILITATION®
CHANGES RESULTS

In Chapter 13, we'll replay the same situation through the lens of a typical Buying Facilitation® conversation. In this case, the vendor will lead the buyer through each issue he needs to address, and each of the systems elements he must include, on the way to a buying decision.

During the chapter:

- We will use Buying Facilitation® to lead the buyer through the systems elements he needs to address before considering a solution;

- We will see how the vendor moves the call forward and gathers the Buying Decision Team from the first call;

- We will identify the differences between facilitating buy-in and influencing a decision, and selling product.

LET'S APPLY A TYPICAL Buying Facilitation® conversation instead of the sales model in Chapter 12.

This conversation will facilitate the hidden, behind-the-scenes issues that Joe needs to manage before he can move forward with a site redesign. Buying Facilitation® will actually teach Joe how to recognize and manage the sometimes unconscious issues in his system so he can get necessary buy-in and proceed to a purchase.

As you read through the dialogue, notice how the vendor (Victoria) leads Joe through stuff he couldn't necessarily know would come up. Notice how there is no real pitch or product discussion.

As Victoria helps Joe maneuver down the decision phases, notice how natural it is. Notice how she leads Joe sequentially through each of the decision phases and through each step of the buying decision cycle. In Chapter 15, I'll break apart each element in the dialogue. For now, just note that it seems so effortless and simple.

Indeed, Victoria takes on the role of a neutral navigator while Joe takes her along his route with him. Joe would be able to get where he's going to end up eventually, as you saw, in 36 weeks.

As you'll see, Joe can do it so much more efficiently with Victoria leading him down his own route, a route that was unknown to him at the start of his discovery process. Ultimately, Joe not only gets where he needs to be faster and easier, but there is better implementation, buy-in and less disruption. And Victoria gets more business.

Note of caution: As you read, notice that Buying Facilitation® effortlessly leads the buyer through all of the systems issues he must manage and resolve before he can make a purchase.

In the dialogue, the contact-to-purchase time was reduced to 12 weeks; the vendor ended up with a larger, quicker sale, and the buyer ended up resolving his problem much earlier, with less political fallout, and with a better solution. Win-win.

What we're doing here is not typical in the sales process. Notice how Victoria avoids falling into the sales traps during those times it would be natural to gather information, pitch, sell, or have answers, and instead helps the buyer manage his decision process.

Note that because the sales model is so ingrained in our thinking that the case study might seem impossible. But when my clients learn Buying Facilitation®, they've had these conversations, with these sorts of results, for over 20 years.

THE BUYING FACILITATION® DIALOGUE

This dialogue will take place on the first call that Joe makes to Victoria. Note how Victoria gets to Joe's buy-in issues immediately: these first Facilitative Questions help them both ascertain if Joe is a real prospect. Along the way, Victoria teaches Joe the sorts of issues he must manage well before he had even realized he'd need to do those things, thereby speeding up the buying decision process.

As a result of the type of leadership Victoria provides, she gets on Joe's decision team quickly. Note the entire discussion is leading Joe through the type of change he must manage: This is not a product sale—and yet a product sale can easily occur once all of this is managed. Victoria is actually teaching Joe what he has to do to achieve his goals with his colleagues, and open up the possibility of her being a solution provider.

Joe calls a local Google listing for a Web Designer.

Joe: I'd like to speak with someone who can provide me with information about doing a web design for a $15 million company.

Victoria: I can help. My name is Victoria. Who am I speaking with please?

Joe: I'm Joe. Are you one of the designers?

Victoria: I am. Do you have some time to speak now or should we make an appointment to do this at a more convenient time. We'll need at least 30 minutes because I'm going to have a lot of questions.

Joe: We can do this now. Do you want information about the company? About our current site?

Victoria: Not yet, but I will a bit later. Can you tell me something about how you currently get your site designed and administered?

JOE: Sure. We have a tech team. They've been handling it for about four years now. But I think it's time for us to get more professional so I'm seeking a vendor who specializes in site design. I saw your stuff on the net and was impressed.

VICTORIA: Thanks! So glad you liked it. We are happy with our results also. I'm wondering what's causing you to consider an outside vendor when your tech folks wouldn't be thrilled giving up a job they've been doing for years. It must be a part of their work load.

JOE: I'm not sure about any of it. I haven't spoken with them yet. I thought I'd speak with a few of my business partners and get the lay of the land before speaking with the techies. I don't think they can handle it or I wouldn't be calling you.

VICTORIA: Do me a favor? Can we put that question on a parking lot?

How will you know that it would be viable to use an outside vendor when the current tech team has historically done all of the site design?

That question will come up when you sit down with the tech team. Not only would they have to give up some of their work, they'd have to support an external group and work together with them. Not necessarily a happy situation. Not to mention that people in your company have gotten used to them, and they are probably doing projects with a lot of the internal teams. It's a very sensitive subject. So let's get that down on paper and we can come back to it once I ask a few more questions.

JOE: I'm relatively new—only been here for eight months, so I inherited them. And I really think they are so inexperienced at the more sophisticated aspects of web design that it's actually harming our business.

VICTORIA: And since you haven't spoken with them yet, you're assuming they won't be able to prove to your satisfaction that they can do better, or you wouldn't be calling me.

JOE: I am assuming that, but of course I'm going to have to give them a chance to prove themselves. They haven't excited me yet, but I do have to give them that chance.

VICTORIA: And it appears that the others on your decision team haven't minded their output or you all would have started looking for a new vendor before today.

JOE: Right. Most of the partner groups don't talk to each other—you know the normal marketing/sales rift, and the brand manager thinks he's above us all. I don't think anyone wanted to tackle the problem, because it's been good enough until now.

VICTORIA: And what made you stop believing it was no longer 'good enough'?

JOE: I've been closely following our daily, weekly, and monthly hits, as well as those of our competitors, and noticing that we are beginning to trail. Not to mention that we aren't doing SEO and adwords and social networking. We've got a lot to do to have us catch up, and I think it's time now.

VICTORIA: So you want a site redesign, you haven't spoken to your tech team, and your Buying Decision Team hasn't started working together yet to determine what they might want to do, or even if they want to do anything different. And none of you know how to work together. Given all that, *I wonder how the team will know how to collaborate around bringing in a new vendor when you all haven't been able to work together on anything else?*

JOE: I'll have to do a presentation and get their attention, and I'll have to get their agreement to start moving forward. I think if I just stress that we need to form a collaborative group to get the best site design for us all, they'll buy in. But they aren't the biggest hurdle. We'll have to get agreement from the CFO because there is no budget, and because technology reports to her.

Now that I think of it, I guess I'll need the buy-in from the other managers in case we have to get funding out of our individual budgets. I have been trying to get us all on the same page. It's been a challenge.

VICTORIA: I hear that there are a lot of people and departments who have a preference for keeping the tech team doing the work. I also hear you have no history of collaborating with the very groups that would need to buy in to bringing in a vendor. Given the issues you've had with the other departments, *what do you plan on doing differently to get their buy-in to either get agreement from the CFO to use an external vendor, or get her to give you budget, or find a way to get the budget from your colleagues?*

JOE: Haven't gotten that far yet. What do you suggest?

VICTORIA: It's a good thing to realize that until all of the team members buy in to getting a new site design, or using an external vendor, or choosing to use the in-house tech team, the decision will be delayed. Especially if you end up needing the CFO's agreement and you'll need to join forces and provide a unified front to her. So a prior relationship and joint vision is very important.

Let's put a few of these questions on the parking lot.

1. *What will the disparate groups need to know or understand to decide to work together?*

2. *How will the group know that a site redesign will provide the outcomes that you assume it will?*

3. *What will each group need to gain to know it would be worth their time and effort?*

JOE: That's a good start for me.

VICTORIA: We'll also need to figure out a business case so you can find funding in case your CFO won't give you funds and you decide to use an external vendor for all or part of the new site.

I have another question:

What will your CFO need to reconsider or know in order to allow in a new vendor when one of her reports is the tech manager?

JOE: I don't know the answer to that. I just put it on my parking lot. We need the answer to that, don't we? She really protects him, and I don't see her letting it go—maybe the front end design, but certainly not the implementation and programming. And that's the part that they won't have time to do—I know how backed up they are.

VICTORIA: I suspect she'll try to get the tech team to do it as long as she doesn't have any price or time criteria that would make her think otherwise. She'd need to believe there was a business case for bringing in an outside vendor, or at least believe there was a possibility that the tech guys couldn't do a good enough job to keep up with or surpass the competition. But it seems by her actions with the current site, she hasn't cared about that until now.

JOE: Is there any way that you could create a project in which you would do the web design and they could do the programming? That might make it easier to make that case with her. At least we could have that as a fall back position, although it is not my preference.

VICTORIA: Sure. We could do the web design and your internal folks could do the programming and the testing and the implementation. And we could oversee it as a project.

How would your Buying Decision Team know that we could give you a great design, manage the internal politics given there will probably be competing needs, and work alongside of your tech team in a collaborative way?

JOE: I'm assuming you've done all that before? And you have references?

VICTORIA: We do. And we've been doing a lot of that shared work in this economy. It sounds like a necessary consideration given the background. Sounds like there are a lot of elements inside that wouldn't want a new vendor coming in.

JOE: I need to sit down with the whole group, and sit down with the CFO and ask her some of the questions that we have on our Parking Lot and show her your site. Then I'd need you to come in and talk with us.

VICTORIA: I'd like to know that the entire team—except the tech team, who I think we should have a separate meeting with after everyone else is on board and open to the possibility of bringing in an outsider—would be there, so we can see where we are at.

What would you need from me to help you have the best possibility of getting agreement from your teammates and your CFO to move forward?

JOE: I'd probably want your thoughts about whether or not to have private conversations first with each of them, or to start with the CFO, or to have you in to do a pitch first to get them excited.

VICTORIA: Having me in first wouldn't make sense. If they didn't want to move on it, I would be a reason to object. Let's put together a plan of action. How would you like to do that?

JOE: How 'bout if I come over there, and we put together a plan. I'd be happy to pay you for coaching me through this— I don't want to abuse your time—and then we can figure out the steps we need to take.

CHANGING RESULTS BY FACILITATING DECISIONS

Let me generally run through the skeleton of this dialogue: We will go through it line by line in Chapter 15 so you can better understand exactly what Victoria did and why.

Victoria quickly highlighted the issues Joe would have to handle as he started on his journey to getting a better website. She collapsed the time element from the first conversation in Chapter 12 by helping Joe understand exactly what needed to happen at a systems and change management level.

Did you notice that soon, Joe began saying 'We?'

Did you notice that Victoria uses Facilitative Questions to teach Joe how to bring together all decision elements? As we saw in the last chapter, without managing these elements, at best Joe would have a much longer decision cycle (as we saw above); at worse, he'd lose his initiative altogether.

Of course we saw in the initial role play how vulnerable the whole initiative was.

Looking at the entire system, Victoria has a choice: She can stand back and let Joe get on with his process, or she can lead him through the issues in the system that need to buy-in for a product purchase to be made. From you.

Because Victoria has a history of working in this environment, she knows the probable systems elements Joe will need to include on his way to a buying decision.

The criteria here are to make it possible for Joe to know how to obtain early, easy buy-in, manage any work-around issues, and plot a path forward.

Follow on activities:

1. Joe meets with Victoria for two hours and puts a road map together to handle each piece of the buying decision and get the Buying Decision Team on board.

2. Joe meets with each member of the team individually and poses the following Facilitative Questions to obtain interest for a project.

a. What would we need to do differently in order to get the sort of website that would put us in a competitive position against our competitors?

b. Given that we have a tech team who has a history of doing our web design, how would we know that we are prepared to wait until they have time to design and implement a new one for us?

c. Given that our tech team has not given us a more professional site until now, how would we know up front that it would be worthwhile to depend on them to give us a highly competitive site? Or to provide our customers with a place to dialogue with us? Or the means to track traffic?

d. How do we move forward to ensure that the CFO will give us the funds and agreements we need to get a site that would enhance our place in the market?

e. How do we know what criteria we need to meet in order to get the best site? Is money a criterion? Time? Competition? And once we decide, how do we work together to get buy-in from the CFO?

f. If we have a time criterion, we'd have to use an external vendor because our tech team couldn't do it in a reasonable time frame.

3. By using these types of questions, and with the support of the vendor to manage each of the strategic and tactical points they need covered, Joe was able to align the team after one meeting, and get them to buy in to a presentation with the CFO about what they wanted from a website, from a vendor, and from the tech team.

4. The team decided they wanted an external vendor to do the entire project, with the tech team just managing the documentation and follow-on support.

5. The team met with the tech group, found out that they were six months behind with their work, and had no knowledge of SEO or Sales 2.0 tools.

6. The team met once with Victoria and one other vendor, choosing Victoria because she was more aware of their issues, familiar with the team, understood the need for collaboration, and they knew that she had helped Joe with the great questions.

7. The team met with the CFO and did a massive presentation on the outcomes, time critical elements, and cost/benefit analysis of hiring an outside vendor to do the whole thing. She refused to fund the initiative, and demanded the use of the in-house team as much as possible for testing, programming, or research if the decision team decided to bring in a web design vendor.

8. The decision cycle took three months; it might have taken less time if Victoria had been contacted earlier.

WRAP UP

By using Buying Facilitation® on the first call, Victoria helped Joe recognize many of the issues he'd need to address—many of which he hadn't even realized at the start. Because he was new to this type of situation, and Victoria was familiar with the sorts of issues people in his position generally had to manage (i.e. because of her knowledge of the field, she was familiar with the probable systems issues), Joe was able to bring forward many problems and considerations he couldn't have known on his own until he'd stumbled on them.

Victoria used each phase of the sequenced decision cycle, through each idea, initiative, relationship, budget issue, that the system might resist or object to, and from there, down the steps to getting buy-in from teammates quickly.

As a result, the entire process was easier for Joe and his team-mates, quicker, more direct, and more targeted, with clearer under-standing of the full range of issues within the Identified Problem and a greater chance for success. And Victoria was the coach and support, leading Joe through his change issues and while maintain-ing the integrity of his system. She did it by serving his decision process, not by supplying a solution. She barely pitched. And yet her solution was built into his decision.

In the next chapter, let's look at both selling models from Victoria's viewpoint.

CHAPTER FOURTEEN

MANAGING THE BUYER'S DECISION: THE VENDOR'S STORY

In Chapter 14, the vendor will tell her story, first from the viewpoint of the typical sales process, and then as a Buying Facilitator. The frustrations and possible lost sales are obvious when just the problem/need scenario is the focus; the difference in the progression of the relationship and buying decision possibilities are obvious in the Buying Facilitation® model.

During the chapter:

■ We'll recognize the frustration of the sales person while trying to sell from proposed need with no understanding of the systems issues involved in the buying decision;

■ We'll recognize the differences between the conventional sale and a facilitated buying decision in the relationship, the sales cycle, and the potential for a closed sale.

IN THE LAST TWO CHAPTERS, we viewed the case study from the buyer's perspective, with a good peek into the sorts of decisions and relationship problems we're not usually privy to. We got to watch how the necessary levels of buy-in got managed, as well as the relationships, the confusion and all around crazy stuff that had to be managed in order for the buyer's system to be willing to change.

I'm also sure you noticed how initially Joe had no consistent criteria for 'success' or 'excellence.' Everyone seemed to be in their own little world, with no special way to work together for the good of the company, not to mention no one even realized there was a problem.

Indeed, until very late in the decision cycle, there were no criteria for how to choose a vendor, which was especially disconcerting since the vendors had already done two presentations based on how they could address the perceived need without understanding how they'd be chosen.

This happens all the time—and we go along, haplessly thinking that if we understand needs, earn trust, and have a great product to present, we'll be a viable choice.

I hope it was obvious how mysterious this was for the buyer, who had no idea when he started where he'd eventually end up. I hope it was equally obvious that doing a sales job and attempting to understand the buyer's needs would not have helped Victoria sell, nor helped the buyer buy.

In this chapter, we'll walk with Victoria down the vendor's path—in the first sales scenario, and then again in her role as a decision facilitator.

In the conventional sales situation Victoria was lucky to have been chosen; she certainly was not chosen on her solution per se. In the Buying Facilitation® dialogue, Victoria became a servant leader and neutral navigator, got onto the Buying Decision Team, and helped the buyer's unconscious, unknown, and absolutely vital future decisions get made effortlessly and early enough in the process to involve the other team members early on.

Enjoy this chapter. It will give you good insights into what you're going through in sales, and show you another possibility.

THE FRUSTRATION OF THE VENDOR—A TYPICAL SALES SITUATION

How Typical Consultative Sales Would Manage This Situation

Your name is Victoria Tabor, and you own a web design company. You specialize in creating and maintaining sites for corporations.

You received a call from a prospect—so nice when the calls come in! Joe is from a smallish manufacturing company. He asked you to come in and give a presentation about what you could offer. He was very accommodating: He was willing to set up a face-to-face appointment for you to come in and gather data, to make sure that you were going to present exactly what they needed.

You visited Joe's site, and spent a good hour with him, hopefully exhibiting your professionalism. Here are questions you needed answered:

1. What did their current website do for them? What more did they need?

2. What more would they like their site to do for them in the way of:

   a. branding themselves and their product;

   b. increasing their presence: on blogs, at the top of search engines;

   c. bringing in new customers;

   d. selling product online;

   e. differentiating themselves from the competition;

   f. creating a social space for customers to discuss their experiences and ask for what they need;

   g. enhancing the message of the company, and start motivational conversations that would position the company as an innovative brand for the future.

3. Is Joe the buyer? Who is the executive sponsor? Who are the decision makers on the project? How does the decision get made?

4. Who else are they considering for the job?

(Private note: the data were given to the three vendors who asked for it.)

Along the way, you learn about Joe's frustration with the current site design and the internal tech group, and why he doesn't want them to do it anymore. It should be easy to prove to them that your site designs are better than the current one.

You also find out that your regular local competitors have also been invited to present. But you had such a good meeting with Joe that you think you have the edge. After all, your site designs have won awards. You're the best.

You presented to Joe the next week. Following your presentation, you were told you'd hear from Joe in about a month. After two months waiting to hear from him, you start calling to find out what's up. Joe says that he's not quite ready to make a decision, and that you'd have to come in and meet more people in a month or so. Good. You made it to the next round.

When you go in for the second presentation, there are more managers there. You expected to see the sales and branding managers, and were a bit surprised that the tech manager came as well. That can't be good—he probably will want to compete with you, steal your ideas, and prove that he can do the job better. You wonder if he's attending the other vendor's presentations as well. And you have no idea how much data about your ideas to reveal.

Following the second presentation, Joe again tells you he'll call you back in a month. You don't hear from him, and call after six weeks to find out if you got the job. Joe doesn't return your call. You wait another month and call again. Joe still doesn't return your call. Shoot. Looks like you lost the job.

Five months after your last presentation, Joe calls you to come in again. Thank goodness you're still in the running. This time you put together a very specialized presentation that shows exactly how you would increase business. And just to add something new, you throw in one power point explaining how you'd work with a team, just in case the tech team ended up being involved in some way.

Two weeks later you get the job! It isn't the job you had hoped for: They only want you to do site design, oversee the tech team's implementation, and be there when it goes live. So it's only a fraction of the business. But you're glad you got chosen.

Sales Discussion

As the chosen vendor in this scenario:

1. You had three presentations over nine months and weren't chosen until weeks after the final presentation.

2. Your presentation was focused on your service without having begun a leadership relationship with the prospects.

3. When you put the presentation material together, you had no way of knowing that their number one criterion would be your ability to collaborate and communicate. Your presentation materials and info gathering was based on their need for a professional corporate design. You got lucky by throwing in that one power point. Had you known, you would have done most of the power points around your history of being part of client teams.

4. You have been offered no choice but to do only the web design part of the job.

5. For your project, you only have access to the in-house tech team and Joe, the marketing manager. All innovation and decisions would be filtered one level down.

A TYPICAL DECISION FACILITATION SCENARIO

How Buying Facilitation® Would Manage This Situation

Your name is Victoria Tabor, and you own a web design company. You specialize in creating and maintaining sites for corporations.

You get a call from Joe, and begin by helping him figure out all of the elements he needs to address. The first discussion point is about the tech team: You know that companies would much rather use their in-house suppliers or familiar vendors than go find a new vendor. Since there is already a website, there must be some sort of web design or tech team that they have been using.

You understand that until Joe and his team figure out if the current tech people will handle the situation, you don't want to spend time putting together a presentation.

You also know there are more decision makers than Joe. There is no need to present until you can get the whole together, and they are ready, willing, and able—with budget—to choose an outside vendor.

You must help Joe figure out how to manage the relationships with his teammates and help them work together, plan together, and coordinate efforts to engage and influence the CFO if they decide to seek an external solution. There must be so many internal politics involved between the sales, marketing, branding, and customer service groups!

You would imagine that given the symmetry between these groups, they would be working together regularly. But you know that if they don't figure out a way to work together, they will start playing games and use company politics to leverage against each other. So you lead Joe into helping the managers work together.

Once the team knows how to work together, they must decide if the current vendor, in this case the tech team, is going to do the work. Until or unless they come up with a joint decision to choose an external vendor, they will continue using their in-house tech team.

One more thing. You want to become part of Joe's Buying Decision Team. If he starts relying on you to help him—and the team—make the sorts of decisions they need to make to get to some level of excellence, you will have proven yourself to be a leader and be relied on to help with other tech decisions. Sure, you'd get more work, but you'd also get a new referral: Joe would be willing to do a video referral for your site.

Buying Facilitation® discussion:

1. Victoria is on the Buying Decision Team from the first call.

2. There was no need for Victoria to put together a presentation before the whole team had decided to investigate an external supplier.

3. Joe agreed to hire Victoria to help him garner team buy-in: If the team didn't buy in, or if the CFO wouldn't go outside the system, Victoria would have gotten paid for her time and would have been saved three unwarranted presentations.

4. Victoria understood the difficulties and the probabilities of the sale on the first call.

5. Victoria and Joe spoke regularly. When Victoria finally presented, she knew the decision team's criteria for choosing a vendor. She did not have to make a presentation solely based on her solution but was able to weight the presentation around her ability to collaborate. She entered as the favored vendor: She was part of the Buying Decision Team from the beginning.

6. In her first call with Joe, there was no pitch: The entire conversation facilitated Joe's buying decision. It was unbiased, and led Joe through each of his decision points: Where are you/What's missing; How can you fix the problem with a familiar solution; What elements need to be included to ensure that the system will remain intact once the solution is adopted?

USING SALES METHODS

When sellers use sales methods, it's impossible for them to lead buyers through all aspects of their buying criteria. And, left to their own devices, the buyer rarely knows the complete set of criteria until the middle of the buying decision.

In this case study, there was no way for anyone to know if this project would allow an external vendor in to provide a new solution. If:

- the management team couldn't work together, decide together, and present together,

- the management team couldn't figure out a way to share budget,

- the tech team ended up doing all of the project,

- the CFO wouldn't agree to a site redesign at this time,

- the CFO wouldn't offer budget or all allow managers to find their own funding, and

- the tech team didn't want to collaborate and made a fuss with the CFO, there would have been no job. And Victoria would have made two or more presentations unnecessarily—wasting all of that time and effort.

None of this could have been understood upfront. Unfortunately, sellers are brought in to present too early in a project, and end up waiting while the buyer figures out how to manage what cannot be known at the start of the project idea. And the seller's time is wasted—often.

Remember: An Identified Problem (in this case, the inadequate web presence) is already an integral, accepted part of the culture before being recognized as problematic. So there is no 'need' per se or they would have fixed it already.

Sellers are brought in to present too early in a project, and end up waiting while the buyer figures out how to manage what cannot be known at the start.

We must also remember that until all of the systemic elements that have created and maintain the system are ready, willing, and able to manage the change, no decision to fix a problem will take place. No matter how large or important the need, as we perceive it. And no matter how determined we are that we should be fixing the need with our solution.

Indeed, we've factored all of this failure into our sales approach until now, and, like with any system, have worked around the inadequacies and made accommodations to the low close rates and long sales cycles. Indeed we have developed more and more work-arounds through the years. But it's broken. And we have a way to fix it.

In Chapter 15, we'll break down each aspect of the facilitative dialogue between Joe and Victoria to understand how the model created the results, and why. We'll also understand what she said to get onto the Buying Decision Team, and how she remained in the decision facilitation process before pitching.

Compared to sales, it might look too good to be true. Think about what you would have done, and where that would have gotten you. And see how facilitating the change management process gets you farther, faster—and gets the buyer farther, faster!—than using the typical sales tools.

LEADING THE BUYER THROUGH
THE BUYING PROCESS

In Chapter 15 we'll break down the skills of Buying Facilitation® by explaining each step of the dialogue—what happened and why—and how the decision facilitation model actually taught the buyer how to manage his systems issues.

During the chapter:

- We'll learn how to use the buyer's natural decision phases to help them come up with their own best answers;

- We'll learn how to use Facilitative Questions and parking lots and Presumptive Summaries to help buyers come up with their own answers;

- We'll lead the buyer through the internal issues he'll have to address, based on understanding systems and successful buying environments;

- We'll see the difference between the process involved with a solution sale and a facilitated buy.

NOW THAT WE are acquainted with the scenario, the problems, and the possibilities, let's break apart the entire Buying Facilitation® dialogue and better understand how Victoria facilitated Joe's ability to influence his team, and made a bigger sale than she would have without this model.

Once again, remember that buyers have to do all of this anyway—and they can do it with you or without you. With you means that you will have some influence on what happens, teach your buyer how to manage all of the issues he might not have realized needed to be managed, get onto the Buying Decision Team, and be a servant leader to your buyer. Not to mention close faster, close more, and make the process much easier on yourself.

THE BUYING FACILITATION® DIALOGUE REVISTED

JOE: I'd like to speak with someone who can provide me with information about doing a web design for a $15 million company.

VICTORIA: I can help. My name is Victoria. Who am I speaking with please?

JOE: I'm Joe. Are you one of the designers?

VICTORIA: I am. Do you mind if we spend some time speaking? I've got a bunch of questions to ask, and am happy to make an appointment to do this at a more convenient time. We'll need at least 30 minutes.

Victoria begins the process of getting into rapport by getting into collaboration and agreement to start, immediately letting Joe know he's in good hands: She respects his time, and takes a leadership role, and immediately begins the process of helping Joe figure out the issues he'll need to manage internally before he could consider purchasing anything from her. Joe knows what Victoria is selling and there is no need for her to discuss her solution until later when/if the decision team agrees to move forward.

Victoria is also managing the direction of the conversation; by taking it over, Joe becomes the responder rather than the questioner. This gives her the control to maneuver Joe through each stage of his decision phases, some of which had not yet been considered.

To do that, she needs to get him to detach, somewhat, from his biases so he can begin the process of seeing the entire landscape of issues in front of him and starting to make some of the decisions he needs to make. If these don't get made—and Victoria can't do it for him of course—she would end up wasting her time pitching, presenting, and following up for a long time.

JOE: We can do this now. Do you want information about the company? About our current site?

VICTORIA: Not yet. I will though. But a bit later. Can you tell me something about how you currently get your site designed and administered?

Victoria has just taken control of the conversation, and begun the process of keeping Joe on track, working one small bit at a time to begin to get him into a more observer mind set, while gathering the bits of systems data she needs to formulate her facilitating questions. Everything he wants to share with her will be heard in time.

This first query addresses the first stage of the buying decision cycle:

Rule 1

Until the prospect can see/understand the full range of systems elements that live congruently within their culture, an Identified Problem is not seen as something that is ready to be resolved—regardless of the cost to the system.

Victoria begins by asking a question about the status quo. She needs them both to understand how the Identified Problem is maintained in the system so she can begin leading him through the elements he needs to start considering on his way to getting his team's buy-in to choose her solution.

It will be obvious to both Victoria and Joe that if the site design has not been updated until now, there are internal, political issues keeping it in place that will need to be influenced. At this point, Joe cannot see all of the issues that need to shift because the current site design—the Identified Problem— is being accepted in the system as being 'fine.' And Joe is just one member of the Buying Decision Team. He cannot get a new web design brought on his own and must discover all of the people and policies that have maintained the current design.

From this first question, Victoria will learn if Joe is working on his own, if there is a regular tech vendor to do an upgrade, and if this group can do the work for Joe. If this group can handle Joe's need, she also needs to know why he's calling her, and what is stopping him (and the others) from continuing to use this group to do the site redesign.

How viable is using the current tech team? How ready are the other members of the Buying Decision Team to act on upgrading the site, if they haven't bothered until now?

If there is a huge bias to continue using the group that has done all of the work until now, or if the collegial network doesn't want to change and she can't help Joe and the Buying Decision Team re-examine how the current system has maintained their status quo, she's probably not got a shot at the business.

JOE: Sure. We have a tech team. They've been handling it for about four years now. But I think it's time for us to get more professional so I'm seeking a vendor who specializes in site design. I saw your stuff on the net and was impressed.

VICTORIA: Thanks! So glad you liked it. We are happy with our results also. I'm wondering how your tech folks are going to handle giving up a job they've been doing for years. It must be a part of their work load.

Victoria poses Facilitative Questions to help Joe determine the issues he'll have to manage, starting with how to change the system by getting buy-in from his colleagues. It seems like she's going to have to compete against the internal tech team—bad odds for an unknown vendor.

She understands that the system will attempt to hang on to their current provider, especially if it turns out that no one has ever challenged the current tech provider before.

Rule 2

Until the prospect explores all obvious, familiar ways to find a solution without choosing a new vendor or product, they will make no decision to buy anything new.

JOE: I'm not sure about any of it. I haven't spoken with them yet. I thought I'd speak with a few of my business partners and get the lay of the land before speaking with the techies.

This is trouble. Joe needs to know this. All of the business partners must be on board, and the high ranking decision makers who originally gave the tech team the responsibility to design and maintain the site are going to have to come to a new decision. And everyone is going to have to take the tech team into consideration as part of their decision process.

VICTORIA: Do me a favor? Let's put that question on a parking lot, because it will be one of the questions you might need to address when you sit down with them. Not only are they going to be giving up some of their work, they'll have to support an external group and work together with them. Not necessarily a happy situation. Not to mention that people in your company have gotten used to them, and they are doing successful projects with a lot of the internal teams. It's a very sensitive subject. So let's get that down on paper and we can come back to it once I ask a few more questions.

Several things have happened here.

1. *Victoria began teaching Joe about the work he's going to have to do internally.*

2. *She is proving herself to be a real asset—Joe doesn't know any of this yet (although as you saw, he'd find out soon enough) and she's saving him time and giving him perspective.*

3. *She's proving that she really cares about Joe's issues, and is using her time to serve him rather than pitch her product.*

VICTORIA: What has caused you to determine that an outside vendor would give you more capability than your current tech team? They must have been doing a good job if you have kept them for four years.

Victoria must ask a question after giving that mini lecture to maintain control of the Buying Decision Funnel. Otherwise Joe would start getting into the company politics and more detail than either of them need now. And her question here is very important: Joe and the Buying Decision Team absolutely must know how to NOT CHOOSE their current vendor; the tech team is currently the familiar resource and chosen vendor.

JOE: I'm relatively new—only been here for eight months, so I inherited them. And I really think they are so inexperienced at the more sophisticated aspects of web design that it's actually harming our business.

VICTORIA: And since you haven't spoken with them yet, you're assuming they won't be able to prove to your satisfaction that they can do better, or you wouldn't be calling me.

JOE: I am assuming that, but of course I'm going to have to give them a chance to prove themselves. They haven't excited me yet, but I do have to give them that chance.

Here is a very important fact: As suspected, the tech team is the favored vendor (All familiar resources are chosen first, remember.) Victoria has to help Joe and the rest of his currently-non-existent team understand their choice criteria.

Obviously everyone else seems to be comfortable-enough with the current site. She needs to help Joe get the appropriate people to either change their criteria for site design, or change their criteria around the sorts of results a different design would give them. At this point, there is no way to know if the tech team can develop a better site, or if they have the time to do it. And there is no way of knowing the budget issues.

Victoria has moved to the final decision phase. Victoria really must help Joe get the other decision makers onto a functioning team that can figure out how to make sure everyone gets what they need and avoid fallout if an external design team comes into the company. Otherwise, there really is no job here for her.

Rule 3

Until or unless all elements of the systems that touch the Identified Problem have bought-in to a new element entering the system, nothing will happen for fear of systems imbalance or systems disruption.

VICTORIA: And it appears that the others on your decision team haven't minded their output or you all would have started looking for a new vendor before today.

JOE: Right. Most of the partner groups don't talk to each other—you know the normal marketing/sales rift, and the brand manager thinks he's above us all. I don't think anyone wanted to tackle the problem because it's been good enough until now.

This is an obvious problem that Joe will have to manage. Victoria can lead him through the process, but he will have to bring them all on board before the project can begin.

VICTORIA: And what made you stop believing it was no longer 'good enough'?

This will help both Joe and Victoria get Joe's buying criteria.

JOE: I've been closely following our daily, weekly, and monthly hits, as well as those of our competitors, and noticing that we are beginning to trail. Not to mention that we aren't doing SEO and adwords and social networking. We've got a lot to do to catch up, and I think it's time now.

VICTORIA: So you want a site redesign, you haven't spoken to your tech team, and your Buying Decision Team hasn't started working together yet to determine what they might want to do, or even if they want to do anything different. And none of you know how to work together. Given all that, I wonder how the team will know how to work together to determine if they think it's time to bring someone new in?

Victoria has just given Joe a tactical overview of all that he must accomplish before he can bring in a new vendor. It's very tactical. But the last Facilitative Question is vital: Joe must get the team to work together to make a new set of decisions.

JOE: I'll have to do a presentation and get their attention. Of course I'll have to get their agreement to start moving forward. I think if I just stress that we need to form a collaborative group to get the best site design for us all, they'll buy in. But they aren't the biggest hurdle. We'll have to get agreement from the CFO because there is no budget, and because technology reports to her.

Now that I think of it, I guess I'll need the buy-in from the other managers in case we have to get funding out of our individual budgets. I have been trying to get us all on the same page. It's been a challenge.

Ah. Another wrinkle! Joe needs to get several levels of buy-in from the other departments and the CFO. They will all have to approve of the project, the funding, and the implementation group.

VICTORIA: I hear that there are a lot of people and departments who have a preference for keeping the tech team doing the work. Given the issues you've had with the other departments, what do you plan on doing differently to get their buy-in to either get agreement from the CFO to work outside the tech team or get her to give you budget?

Joe absolutely needs the answer to this. He's got nowhere to go otherwise, and his desire for a better site will come to nothing.

JOE: Haven't gotten that far yet. What do you suggest?

Joe has just put Victoria on the Buying Decision Team. She's become his coach. And indeed she's been coaching him all the way through.

VICTORIA: It's a good thing to realize that until all of the team members buy in to getting a new site design, or using an external vendor, or choosing to use the in-house tech team, the decision will be delayed. Especially if you end up needing the CFO's agreement and you'll need to join forces and provide a unified front to her. So a prior relationship and joint vision is very important.

Let's put a few of these questions on the parking lot. 1. how will the team decide to work together; 2. how will they know that doing the redesign will actually bring in more money (I bet the CFO will like that one), and 3. what will each group want to walk away with to ensure that it will be worth their time and effort.

Victoria is doing a fine tactical coaching job. And Joe trusts her. No reason not to: Her ideas are sound, and every comment is directed toward helping him make his best decisions. And there is no manipulation going on; at no point is Victoria setting Joe up and wending her way back to her product. She is really, truly, serving the client.

Note that by now, she's only 20 minutes in to the first conversation. If this is going to work, Joe has a lot to do on his end to gather the folks who need to buy-in to using an external vendor. If it's not, Victoria doesn't want to waste her time.

JOE: That's a good start for me.

VICTORIA: We'll also need to figure out a business case in case your CFO won't give you any money and you decide to use an external vendor for all or part of the new site.

I have another question: How will your CFO decide to allow in a new vendor when one of her reports is the tech manager?

They must have the answer to this or there is nowhere to go.

JOE: I don't know the answer to that. I just put it on my parking lot. We need the answer to that, don't we? She really protects him, and I don't see her letting it go—maybe the front end design, but certainly not the implementation and programming. And that's the part that they won't have time to do—I know how backed up they are.

VICTORIA: I suspect she'll try to get the tech team to do it so long as she doesn't have any price or time criteria that would make her think otherwise. She'd need to believe there was a business case for bringing in an outside vendor, or at least believe there was a possibility that the tech guys couldn't do a good enough job to keep up with or surpass the competition. But it seems by her actions with the current site, she hasn't cared about that until now.

These are very important tactical points. Victoria is laying out the systems issues she understands (of course she can't understand the content—the specifics—because she doesn't live in Joe's company). Note that she's making a case as to why they can't bring in a new vendor. And it's a valid point. She is actually helping Joe determine what needs to be considered internally before knowing whether he CAN or CANNOT choose an external vendor. He's going to do this anyway—with her or without her. She'd much rather know now than after several presentations.

JOE: Is there any way that you could create a project in which you would do the web design and they could do the programming? That might make it easier to make a case with her. At least we could have that as a fall back position.

VICTORIA: Sure. We could do the web design and your internal folks could do the programming and the testing and the implementation. And we could oversee it as a project.

This is not what Victoria wants—a piece of a job. Not to mention the frustration of working with an in-house team that has other time constraints and resentment that they didn't get the whole job. But she's got to be where Joe is and lead him beyond that. So Victoria has to have Joe really look at that decision from an unbiased viewpoint.

VICTORIA: How would your Buying Decision Team know that we could give you a great design, manage the internal politics given that there may be competing needs, and work alongside your tech team collaboratively?

Victoria is now at the point where it's time to have Joe discuss how he'd choose her. She's proven her leadership skills; she's gotten Joe's trust as he uses her to help him make decisions; Joe now clearly knows the work he's got to do, and he knows how they'd have to position her with the rest of the Buying Decision Team (which doesn't even exist yet).

JOE: I'm assuming you've done all that before? And you have references?

VICTORIA: We do. And we've been doing a lot of that shared work in this economy.

What would you and your decision team, including the CFO, need to know from or about us, to know that it might be worthwhile to have a conversation?

Notice that Victoria did not leave her direct response without adding a question: If she just responded without adding the question, Joe would be in control of the conversation.

Victoria is willing to do a presentation—but only to the entire team. And of course, Joe may not be able to put together the team. If he can, it's an indication that they are willing to look outside for a solution. If not, she will have spent 30 minutes on a call and really helped someone think through his choices, and saved herself a year's worth of following a prospect that is going nowhere.

JOE: First I need to sit down with them all, and sit down with the CFO and ask her some of the questions that we have on our Parking Lot, and show her your site. Then I'd need you to come in and talk with us.

VICTORIA: I'd like to know that the entire team—except the tech team, who I think we should have a separate meeting with, after everyone else is on board and open to the possibility of bringing in an outsider—would be there, so we can see where we are at. What would you need from me to help you have the best possibility of getting agreement from your teammates and your CFO to move forward?

Joe is now formally asking for Victoria's help. She is really clear that she's not going to be involved unless the entire team will be.

JOE: I'd probably want your thoughts about whether or not to have private conversations first with each of them, or start with the CFO, or have you in to do a pitch first to get them excited.

VICTORIA: Having me in first wouldn't make sense—if they didn't want to move on it, I would be a reason to object. Let's put together a plan of action. How would you like to do that?

She's making a sale here. And he's ready to buy.

JOE: How 'bout if I come over there, and we put together a plan. I'd be happy to pay you for coaching me through this— I don't want to abuse your time—and then we can figure out the steps we need to take.

Victoria is assured some work, and a good possibility of being the chosen vendor if that becomes a possibility. She didn't have to go through all of the face visits (This was all done by phone.); she didn't have to wait for 36 weeks; and she isn't in the dark—she knows the entire buying decision process, although of course can't know the day-to-day personal politics and jockeying that will go on.

SUMMARY

I hope it was obvious that there is a difference in the skills between those used by Victoria in the case study above, and the typical sales conversation. Victoria was a true servant leader, and led Joe through all of the decision issues he needed to manage.

Notice how the conversation stayed in the systems-decisions end of the buying decision, not the solution placement end. It actually led Joe through all of the decision issues he was eventually going to have to work through, eventually focusing on the big one:

If there was a choice to bring in an external vendor to do the design work, she would make her sale. Otherwise, Joe would discover right away that it would never happen.

In addition, Victoria actually helped Joe set a course through each of the elements he'd need to manage. If she had concentrated on selling her solution rather than helping maneuver Joe through his change issues, she would have had the same situation as the first sales interaction.

Although Victoria couldn't be in each of the follow-on meetings, and certainly couldn't know the relationships or the personalities, she understood the system of what needed to take place. She helped influence the route through the people and policies, and the job descriptions that would need to be involved for there to be buy-in for a project to move forward. She took a leadership role—a Buying Consultant, or a Buying Facilitator.

Victoria also actually never discussed her solution, and used Buying Facilitation® during the entire conversation to lead the prospect through the range of buying decisions he was going to have to make, including getting partner buy-in, getting the CFO on board early, and getting the tech team to partner instead of being hostile.

Until Joe did all of these things, he couldn't hire a vendor anyway. Indeed, if there was no buy-in from the partner managers, and the CFO wouldn't come up with funding, Joe would have had no way to go outside the system to bring in a new vendor.

As was obvious, the buyer couldn't have known what was going to happen in advance, and the seller was in the dark until the end of the long process. Starting a sale from the point of helping guide the elements included in a buying decision requires new skills, mainly to help a buyer do what needs to happen to choose you.

Just remember, that until or unless the buyer can figure out all that needs to happen before anything can happen, and until there is buy-in, we can't make a sale.

CHAPTER
SIXTEEN

CONCLUSION:
SELLERS CAN MAKE BUYERS SMART

A FRIEND OF MINE called to tell me she had to admit something but not to be annoyed. For six months she had been trying to land a deal with a large local company, and had been to see the management several times to pitch and have working lunches. They were all set to go when she got a call to please go to Minneapolis (in the winter of course) to meet with their new business partner and introduce herself and her product. She flew up, stayed overnight, and spent half a day with them.

She thought they were all good-to-go but then got a call three days later saying that once they did some discovery they realized that one of their partners had a vendor whose solution was similar. They were going to have to go with that vendor for political reasons.

If she had been using Buying Facilitation®, she could have enabled the Minneapolis group's discovery of their other partner before she went up there. In fact, she could have used this question (below) on her colleagues in Austin before she even met the folks in Minneapolis:

What has stopped you from having this issue resolved for you before now? And what can you use from within your normal work environment that could offer you a solution?

By understanding the system—the fact that most companies have vendors that handle the same thing her solution manages—that question should have been one of her first Facilitative Questions when she met the group months before.

But even as she received the bad news, she could have opened up the possibility of using her in addition to the existing vendor. She needed only these Facilitative Questions:

At what point will you know if the other vendor is able to manage the full range of issues you seek to correct?

How would you know that my solution would be a good add-on and would work in tandem with the other vendor to give you a richer solution?

How many times have you lost sales that you spent months or years working on? But now you know that it's possible to get different results, even when it all looks lost.

PUTTING IT ALL TOGETHER

Indeed, for decades low time-to-close ratios have been the norm, with sales folks working hard to close a fraction of the sales they deserve to close, all the while rationalizing their low success ratio. And the field of sales keeps the status quo in place rather than seeking excellence, changing, or recognizing that the model itself is broken.

We've assumed our system was fine—just problematic, and blamed the buyer for not knowing how to buy.

Sales has ignored the first phase of a buying decision. With only a small part of the decision process available to influence, we have attempted to place a solution by understanding need, gathering data, being professional and trustworthy, or having a good solution—the best we could do with what we had.

> With 100 prospects, we close plus or minus seven. And it's a shame.

Unfortunately buyers know what to do with our wonderful information only when they've bought-in to change.

As a result, we've closed the statistical average: With 100 prospects, we close plus or minus seven. And it's a shame: We not only know our solution and capabilities, but we understand the system behind a buyer's environment. We could have been a greater asset to them all along.

Now that we know how to help them manage their change and decision making issues, we can have a whole new set of skills that manage the *beginning* of the buying decision cycle *and then* use our sales skills once the buyer's decision team has determined their full set of criteria for bringing in a solution.

THE DIRTY LITTLE SECRETS

During the course of this book, you have been introduced to all of the Dirty Little Secrets that have caused you to fail far more frequently than you should have.

Let's put everything we've learned together and discuss the twelve Secrets.

1. *Sales focuses on solution placement and has no skill set to help buyers maneuver through their off-line, internal, behind-the-scenes planning and decision making that must take place before they can buy.*

It is impossible for any change to happen (including a purchasing decision) unless a system has identified the elements that need to buy in to the change. Our current sales model has ignored this invisible challenge since its inception. Rather than realize that a piece was missing, it instead builds in assumptions that maintain its status quo, provides work-arounds to manage the fall-out of the one-dimensional approach, and accepts low close ratios.

Now we know all of the elements involved in how buyers buy, and can help them manage both ends of their decision making and change management. We can close sales in half the time since we'll be severely shortening the buying decision cycle.

> *2. Buyers will make no purchasing decisions until they get buy-in from the components (people, policies, initiatives, groups) that are in any way connected to, or adjacent to, their 'need.'*

Because we invariably meet our prospects before they have gone through their change activities and our sales cycle is longer than necessary, we enter at the wrong time, with the wrong focus, and get bad results.

Now we can be a support person at both ends of the buying decision: First, as a decision facilitator; next, as a solution provider. We will be able to help them recognize and manage their decision elements and be put on their Buying Decision Teams early on.

> *3. Until or unless the system is ready, willing, and able to buy in to change, buyers will not accept a solution no matter how great the need.*

The system is sacrosanct. No purchase will be made until the system knows it will maintain integrity, regardless of the cost of not resolving the problem. As sellers we have pushed into the need and ignored the systems-management end of the equation.

Now we can help them get systems buy-in before we offer them a solution. We both will know far more about their 'need' once they understand where any change will fit into their system.

> *4. To insure minimal internal disruption, buyers must do change management before considering a new solution.*

Once a buyer's system knows how to change without facing risks, it is willing to bring in something new. To do that, they must manage their change issues.

Now we can lead them through their change process and help them maneuver through their buying decision issues. Because we now have the skills to remain unbiased, we can navigate a route through their system before discussing our solution.

> 5. *Until buyers understand, and know how to mitigate, the risks that a new solution will bring to their culture, they will do nothing.*

Buyers begin solution discovery prematurely, without first understanding the route they will have to take to get buy-in for any systemic change or purchase.

Now we can help them understand and manage their risks, and get agreement for change and a purchase. If the outcome is not based on their need or our solution. Neither of us will initially understand the route buyers must take to get the systemic buy-in. But our understanding of systems will help them get the right people and initiatives together quickly.

> 6. *Until buyers have managed their internal systems, they have limited ability to use the solution information you would like to give them.*

We've never been taught all of the issues that need to be managed before a buying decision can happen. Our buyers haven't known that either. As a result we have unwittingly focused on solving their problem, giving them vast amounts of data about our solution, and have not realized that buyers haven't known what to do with that data until later on in their buying decision process.

Now we can help buyers discover their systems and change management issues, and help them figure out their buying criteria that will match the values of their system.

> *7. Sales, and the focus on solutions, enters the buyer's decision path too early in their decision cycle.*

Sellers have overlooked the buyer's need to manage the hidden dynamics involved in the buying decision. Now we have two sets of skills: We can enter first as decision facilitators, then become solution providers.

> *8. Helping buyers maneuver through their buy-in and systems issues require a different focus and a different skill set from the one sales offers.*

The typical sales scenario overlooks the systems issues that must seek homeostasis. Focusing on our solutions, we've created the rejections, the objections, the long delays, and the 'dumb' decisions. Not to mention the abysmal closing ratio of under 10% (from first prospecting call).

Now we have the skills to enter the buying decision end of the equation without bias and as a decision facilitator. We can help the buyer focus first on finding all of the right people, discovering the historic precedents, changing the rules, and getting buy-in so they can all figure out what needs to happen to achieve excellence.

> *9. Buyers buy on unique, idiosyncratic criteria that are agreed to by their Buying Decision Team (people not necessarily directly involved with the Identified Problem but having some historic connection), not on the strength of their need, your product or service, or your relationship.*

They buy for reasons that largely have nothing to do with us. And we sell for reasons that largely have nothing to do with them. This fact has kept buyers in their buying decision cycle longer than necessary.

Now we can help the Buying Decision Team discover their criteria so they can resolve their internal systems issues and move forward to a product purchase in approximately one-eighth the length of the sales cycle.

> *10. The type of relationship a seller has with customers and prospects is a buying feature only after the buyers have determined how, when, why, and if they are going to buy.*

Sales has used a 'relationship management' approach as a sales technique, hoping that a good relationship will influence a buying decision. But buyers buy according to how their system manages their change issues.

Now we can help buyers down their decision route and be chosen because of our true consulting skills.

> *11. Information doesn't teach people how to make a buying decision. Learning details of our solution is the last thing buyers need.*

Sales has focused on having the solution to meet the need. As a result, sellers spend time and effort honing the appropriate messages for their pitches, presentations, and marketing. But buyers don't know what to do with the data that early on in their decision process because they haven't managed their buying criteria yet.

Now we can help buyers discern all of their decision criteria and buying criteria. When it's time to pitch or present, we can massage our message to fit with the buying criteria and values.

> *12. Buyers don't initially understand the process they must go through en route to resolving a need.*

Buyers don't realize that when they begin thinking about a solution to a problem, their first forays into solution discussions are premature and their first contacts with sales people are preliminary.

Now we help the buyer assemble the Buying Decision Team and walk down their decision criteria, avoiding objections, delays, and bad decisions. We can close 200-800% more than typical sales. We can now steer them away from their problem and toward the steps they must take to gain acceptance for systems change.

Now we can lead buyers through the route they must take to gather the decision makers and manage the change as they get the necessary buy-in to bring in a solution.

WE ARE ALSO PART OF A SYSTEM

Because sales has not had a skill set to help manage the hidden dynamics behind the change issues, we've sat and waited for sales to close, or lost untold sales unnecessarily, or failed to help perfectly viable prospect know how to choose us. But this, too, is a system.

Indeed, our 'sales' system is very similar to a prospect's buying decision system:

1. We are adding sales skills to the wrong end of the problem.

2. We'd need buy-in from the field, or from our bosses, to change the sales model we've been using.

3. We've been living with the problem for so long we've built in a 90% failure rate as our success.

4. The system continues to maintain itself and recreate the problem daily.

As a result of having missed the change management piece, here are the work-arounds we've not only bought in to our systems, but believe they are necessary.

Need: We've assumed that a buyer has an urgent need that must be resolved by a solution (ours hopefully). We have ignored the fact that their system requires buy-in and change management before their Identified Problem can be resolved.

Sales has a 'need' for a way to help buyers make better, faster decisions and give us good information to work with. It keeps trying to fix the problem with the same components that cause the problem to begin with.

Objection: The buyer's system will reject proposed change or solution information if its system is being challenged to change in a way that would disrupt it.

Sales rejects bringing in tools outside their accustomed skill set because it would upset what has been seen as 'sales.'

Long sales cycle: A buying decision won't take place until all systems issues buy-in to bringing a foreign element into the system. The time it takes buyers to come up with their own answers is the length of the sales cycle.

When they first consider solving a problem buyers don't know which issues will need to be reconfigured, eliminated, or in any way changed on their way to resolving a problem. They have no way to understand the type of solution they will need until all systems issues are managed.

Sales has spent decades trapped in trying harder and harder to manage the solution end. Until it recognizes that there is a missing piece, it will continue facing the same problems regardless of work-arounds and new-new things in the field.

Pitch: We present solution data too early, without recognizing that the system understands data only in relation to why new information is necessary.

Sales has ignored the evidence that it's been failing (even with obvious problems, and poor results proportionately) because it has a basic belief that with good information, a need, and a proper solution, the buyer should buy. The

*system of sales has not been open to adding anything new.
So pitching the need to add a new set of skills will only
be adopted once the sales model understands the need
to manage solution placement.*

"Closing": Sales assumes that with the right solution and the right
vendor, the buyer should buy. Presentations, closing strategies, and
pitches are geared to joining the 'need' to the 'solution'.

*Sales has converged around information: information
gathering, sharing, understanding, presenting, placing,
pitching, and now with Sales 2.0, doing it better and harder
and more. Sadly, information doesn't teach anyone to make
a new decision, and it is ignored if it flies in the face of
what the system believes is true. If information alone could
easily change a system, the system would be vulnerable to
anything new that it came into contact with. So any sort
of closing technique is moot if the system hasn't bought
into change.*

We know now it's not about the need, or the product, or the
solution; the trusted advisor relationship or the needs analysis or
the influencers; the presentation or the relationship or who-knows-
who. It's merely about the decision to change.

HOW DO WE CHANGE?

As a sales person, I now have an entirely different attitude about my
job. Each call is a puzzle to solve, a system to understand, a route to
discover.

I know that as I help buyers go down their path to discovery, they
include me and my solution in to their system and solution design. I
no longer get objections, I no longer have time lags, I no longer wait
in a shroud of mystery as buyers figure out how to get buy-in. I rarely

have to pitch, I never have to do presentations or proposals, and I am differentiated from my competition immediately.

The old issues I had as a seller are no longer there. I have fun, I truly serve my clients with deep integrity, and I'm making a lot more money.

Let me offer a Q & A with questions I frequently get asked:

What is the first thing I need to do? First, change your belief about your job description. You are now responsible for two jobs: 1. helping buyers maneuver through their hidden dynamics to make sure they get buy-in from all appropriate factions surrounding their Identified Problem, and 2. placing product.

Next, change your expectations. There is no need for a 90% failure rate; you should have at least a 40% close rate with all appropriate prospects. You determine prospect appropriateness on the first call and drop immediately the inappropriate prospects who will never be able to get buy-in for change.

What is the new definition of sales? Sales is a set of skills that helps buyers recognize, align, and manage the full spectrum of change and decision issues needed to get buy-in for a proposed modification of their current system. It consists of a decision facilitation skill set to help manage the change end of the decision, and a solution placement set of activities that parallel the buying criteria defined by the Buying Decision Team.

What are the main skill sets? You must understand the system, and how it maintains itself daily, and how decisions can shift systems while managing systems congruence.

A new set of decision facilitation skills is also necessary to lead buyers through a change management journey.

Most importantly, understand the three decision phases, and the 10 steps buyers go through as they move toward a buying decision. Learn how to formulate Facilitative Questions, stay in the coach/observer place on the mountaintop, and remain unbiased as you lead buyers through their search to find all relevant people and policies, rules and historic relationships, which maintain and continue their status quo.

Once they have managed their change risks, place your product in relation to their buying patterns, not your selling patterns.

How is it possible to get such a high success rate? The sales model only handles the solution-placement/need repair end of the buying decision cycle. All of the time we spend trying to help a buying decision take place before all systems are 'go' is a waste of time and actually delays the purchasing decision.

When you help buyers discover quickly all of the people and issues they need to bring in to the discussion, they can start the ball rolling down the right path with the right people, the right discussions, the right concerns to address, and the right things to do in the right order. Buyers had to figure this out on their own until now, and it's been a hunt-and-peck, unconscious, and mysterious process.

How can we give them so much help if we don't understand their needs? In our professional capacity, we know our products and the way they resolve problems. We know what works, and what doesn't work, at a systems level. We know when we hear that two adjacent groups aren't speaking that there is a problem with probable fallout; we know that if the tech team is being left out there is a potential problem; we know that if there is a 50% turnover in a field that has 15% normally, that there is a problem.

By focusing on the system, and trusting that the buyer will do their own part internally to manage the discussions, the meetings, the stakeholder buy-in, while we provide the parameters of activity from the outside, we can get onto the Buying Decision Team as a consultant and change agent.

Once buyers have the right people aboard, they can make the necessary changes and decisions to allow an opening for a new solution.

What is the biggest hurdle I have? As long as we think that a familiar problem could be resolved by our solution, and we begin to gather data about the 'need', we're in trouble.

Of course, understanding the 'need' is imperative once all of the other decisions get made upfront, although many of the details will change and the holes filled in once the right information from the right people has been gathered and the decision criteria set.

But until or unless the buyers come up with their own systemic answers and recognize their route through change, they will take no action regardless of their need.

Why would a stranger engage in this sort of discussion with me if they don't know me, don't know my product, or even need my solution?

Once we begin using Facilitative Questions at the onset of the first call (focus on the buyer's discovery, lead buyers through their systemic issues, focus on change management, and address the hidden dynamics underlying their status quo), they will immediately recognize a servant leader and change agent, rather than a seller.

Remember, buyers need to do this discovery and change management anyway. They are going to do it with you or without you. And the time it takes them to do it is the length of the sales cycle. We can continue doing what we've been doing— sit and wait and hope—and get our typical low close rate. Or we can help them make their decisions and become a part of their team, and close at least 200% more sales.

NO MORE STUPID ANYBODY

We no longer need to be the stupid sellers, waiting for buyers to buy; our buyers no longer need to be stupid, trying to figure out on their own the mystery of fixing a problem and maintaining homeostasis.

We can now offer them a path through their bewildering decisions as they learn how to gather their decision team, understand all of the changes they have to manage, and design a solution that matches their criteria. And after we've provided the route through to these activities, they will know how to choose us quickly. We will close more business, much more easily.

We have worked diligently to become professionals, gather the right information, and present professionally. It's difficult to conceive that we can actually add a new set of skills that will enable us to be even more professional and successful. Adding Buying Facilitation® to our sales skills will give us that cutting edge and enable us to be successful in today's shifting climate.

Now, I hope you'll spend a few moments getting buy-in from your boss so you can begin becoming a decision facilitator—and increase your sales immediately.

RESOURCES

IF YOU WANT to manage the front end of the buying decision process and learn the Buying Facilitation® Method—how to listen for systems, manage change, get Buying Decision Team members together for your second visit/meeting, and formulate the Facilitative Questions and Presumptive Summaries—go to www.buyingfacilitation.com and see what products feel best.

The Guided Study program is a serious immersion into learning the skills of Buying Facilitation® and change management for any environment or situation.

If you'd like to learn more about the Buying Facilitation® Method itself, go to www.buyingfacilitation.com and have a look at my book *Buying Facilitation: The New Way to Sell That Influences and Expands Decisions*. Get two free sample chapters: http://newsalesparadigm.com/salepage/ebooks/BuyingFacilit Sample1.pdf. This book is a companion to *Dirty Little Secrets*.

To learn more about Buying Facilitation® go to:
www.newsalesparadigm.com

To contact Sharon Drew Morgen: sdm@austin.rr.com

To read Sharon Drew's blog: www.sharondrewmorgen.com

To follow discussions around *Dirty Little Secret* go to
www.dirtylittlesecretsbook.com

BIBLIOGRAPHY

Anneke Seley and Brent Holloway, *Sales 2.0: Improve Business Results Using Innovation Sales Practices and Technology* (New York City: Wiley, 2008).

Roger C. and Peter G. Childers Schank, *Tell Me a Story: A New Look at Real and Artificial Memory* (New York City: Scribner, 1990).

Roger C. Schank and Peter Childers, *The Creative Attitude: Learning to Ask and Answer the Right Questions* (New York: Scribner, 1988).

Edgar H. Schein, *Organizational Culture and Leadership*, 3rd edition (San Francisco, CA: Jossey-Bass, 2004).

Denise Shiffman, *The Age of Engage: Reinventing Marketing for Today's Connected, Collaborative, and Hyperinteractive Culture* (Ladera Ranch, CA: Hunt Street Press, 2008).

APPENDIX

THE SECRETS

1. Sales focuses on solution placement and has no skill set to help buyers maneuver through their off-line, internal, behind-the-scenes planning and decision making that must take place before they can buy.

2. Buyers will make no purchasing decisions until they get buy-in from the components (people, policies, initiatives, groups) that are in any way connected to, or adjacent to, their 'need.'

3. Until or unless the system is ready, willing, and able to buy in to change, buyers will not accept a solution no matter how great the need.

4. To insure minimal internal disruption, buyers will do change management before considering a new solution.

5. Until buyers understand, and know how to mitigate, the risks that a new solution will bring to their culture, they will do nothing.

6. Until buyers have managed their internal systems, they have limited ability to use the solution information you would like to give them.

7. Sales, and the focus on solutions, enters the buyer's decision path too early in their decision cycle.

8. Helping buyers maneuver through their buy-in and systems issues require a different focus and a different skill set from the one sales offers.

9. Buyers buy on unique, idiosyncratic criteria that are agreed to by their buying decision team—not on the strength of their need, your product, or their relationship. The typical sales scenario overlooks the systems issues that must seek homeostasis as they examine their choices.

10. The type of relationship a seller has with customers and prospects is a buying feature only after the buyers have determined how, when, why, and if they are going to buy.

11. Information doesn't teach people how to make a buying decision. Learning details of our solution is the last thing buyers need.

12. Buyers don't initially understand the process they must go through en route to resolving a need.

THE FOUNDATIONAL BELIEFS

Here are the basic tenets for helping buyers decide. While there is some overlap, I've categorized each element for reference.

Underlying Laws

1. Buyers live in systems: family systems, corporate systems, relationship systems. Any problem sits comfortably within the system that has created it and maintains it daily.

2. All systems have inherent elements that everyone in the system adheres to, buys in to, and protects, be they functional or dysfunctional. Systems will create work-arounds that keep these elements in place.

3. Until or unless these elements are found lacking, the status quo will keep everything the same regardless of the cost.

4. If something in the system is inadequate, and there is agreement to enhance it, the system will first seek an internal, familiar solution before it can look outside the system for a solution.

5. Once the system realizes that it cannot use a familiar solution, it needs to find an external solution that must get buy-in from those elements touching the Identified Problem.

6. Once the solution enters the system, it must take on the rules of the system.

7. Systems would rather continue operating with a faulty element than face the disruption of the whole system to fix the one faulty element.

New Criteria for Facing Financial/Global Change

Members of the Buying Decision Team must have answers to the following questions before they choose a new solution, whether the economy is doing well or poorly, whether the decision team has been in place a long time or has just been thrown together. Remember that they haven't thought of any of this until now, and they are as confused as we are—maybe more:

- How can they work together effectively with (possibly new) stakeholders that have no political history together? How will they design a new set of cultural norms that will shift the old system rules to the new culture?

- How will they make decisions in an information vacuum and define the negative risks versus the positive risks?

- At what point will they recognize they've gotten the buy-in they need to ensure that following a purchase the system will be stable?

- How will they know when an internal solution/work-around is worth maintaining, or when it's time to seek an external solution?

- How will new staffing patterns and shifting team members affect their ways of working together?

- How can they define and track what success and failure will look like so they can minimize personal risk?

- What sort of risk are they willing to accept?

- How do they reweight priorities without sufficient analytic data?

- How will they understand what has gotten in the way of them resolving the Identified Problem until now?

- How can they maintain the integrity of the system while going through confusion and change?

- How can they minimize risk and include everyone through both the decision making process and the implementation of their choices?

New Beliefs for the Buying Consultant

Here are some rules for the first half of the sales process when the seller becomes a Buying Facilitator:

- Focus on supporting the decisions that need to get made during the buyer's discovery and buy-in process and may have nothing to do with a decision to make a purchase or solve a problem; the solution sale will come after all issues have been addressed. The desire to be the best they can be—the buyer's outcomes that can be achieved with our solution—will be included within the direction of our facilitative conversations.

- Recognize we are in it for the long haul and not a quick sale (although that might happen as we give buyers the tools to manage all of their internal issues quickly).

- Shift our personal success factors: What will success look like if the first portion of the sales process is focused on a decision rather than a closed sale? How will the sale proceed? How will the client conversations go? What are the responsibilities of being on the Buying Decision Team as an outsider?

- The first conversation must focus on helping create collaboration and recognize what and who needs to be included in their steps toward a solution. Until that happens, there will be no agreement to change.

- A sale is composed of a change management model followed by a solution-placement activity.

- Product pitch has no place until the buyer recognizes, manages, and aligns all of their decision criteria.

TIPS

Here are a few tips on using Buying Facilitation® along with your typical sales process:

Rapport

Build rapport. In sales, we've been taught to get into rapport so we can ask cranky, ingratiating questions like: Who is THE decision maker? But that question doesn't help the buyer make a decision.

We've been taught Relationship, Relationship, Relationship. All those relationships. But that is predicated on the assumption that if we're nice, really nice, that buyers will choose us.

But think about it. Everyone is working toward getting into relationships. If that's the criterion a buyer will use to choose, they'll be hard pressed with all of those sales people being so NICE.

I once met another sales 'expert.' We started a very casual email exchange. We ended up sending each other quick notes daily, and he was so so charming, and thoughtful and kind. After about two weeks of this friendly banter, he sent me—out of the blue—a very stylized pitch to join one of his sites as an Expert, and pay only $500/month for the privilege.

I wrote him immediately: "Have you been nice nice nice to me so you could create a 'relationship' and sell to me?" Oh, how silly I was to think that! Yet I never heard from him again. Except two weeks later when I sent him one of our regular jokes, and got no response. I actually picked up the phone and called him in London! "You stopped speaking to me. Is it because I wouldn't buy your product? Is it because you were only being nice so you could have a relationship with me and then I'd buy from you?" "No No' he assured me. He'd been busy, no time, no email, crashed system. And of course I never heard from him again.

Buyers don't want us to be their friend; they want to resolve a business problem. If we can help them, they'll love us. Don't work at being in rapport through being nice, or smart, or having a great product. Do it because we are helping prospects discover how to make their unconscious decision issues conscious, and how to gather the criteria for change and solution design from the very first contact.

Telephone

Don't be in such a rush to get face-to-face with a prospect. Use the telephone for the first steps; the decision facilitation process works as well with a telemarketing call as with a face-to-face meeting with an entire Board of Directors.

The contact is about their decision—not your product. And when the time comes to share product knowledge, a presentation or a face meeting can be perfect if they all decide that is the best route to serve them.

Since neither our solution, our brand, or our sterling personalities are enough to help buyers understand their choice criteria at a first meeting, our first encounters will involve a wholly different skill set and focus. Before now, we actually slowed down the buying decision process by getting prospects to focus on a new solution before it was time.

We know that buyers buy according to their buying patterns. Before now, there have been enough buyers who matched our selling patterns. But we can't play those odds anymore. Now we must eschew our selling patterns and match their buying patterns. Our new jobs are to help the buyer make their buying decisions consciously, and help them bring together the full complement of decision team members as early as possible.

'We' Space'

From the first minute of the call, help the prospect look around their environment to recognize how their status quo is serving them in the area our solution can resolve. Until or unless buyers recognize the systems elements that lie around the Identified Problem and create a work-around, they won't know the route through all decision factors.

Once they begin to recognize all of the elements they need to address, they will understand how to progress toward a solution. As this part has nothing to do with a purchase—but precedes and impedes the purchase—the conversation will proceed in a way that is considerably different from what you're accustomed to.

Maintain the System Elements That Maintain the Status Quo

Help the buyer discover how their status quo works for them. If they don't desire anything different from what they have, nothing will change: they are not buyers. Use Buying Facilitation® to help open up possibility.

Once the buyer determines they want to change, help them search for the work-arounds, internal resources, and external solution providers that might provide a solution. Until they resolve these issues, they will not need a new vendor. (This is a hard one: You're actually pushing buyers to not buy from you! Remember that until they are absolutely certain they cannot, absolutely cannot, use a familiar solution, they will do nothing.)

Help the buyer recognize all of the elements that are tangled together that make it hard to separate the Identified Problem from other elements and that need to be included into the solution design. Include the groups, teams, departments, or people, that touch the Identified Problem in any way—directly or peripherally, past, present, future—and need some sort of input into the buying decision.

Everyone is a decision maker; asking who the decision maker is is like asking who is leading a contra dance. And, the path that the decision takes is mysterious, circuitous, and has no known result until the end.

Pitching

We only pitch as the final stage of a two-phased process:

Phase 1. Help the buyer to recognize and manage the internal issues that have created and maintained the status quo, and to decide how, when, and if to resolve these factors by ensuring the internal elements are ready to adopt something new.

Phase 2. Give the buyer details of how your particular solution will help them manage the above internal issues.

Nothing will happen until these issues are managed.

Remember that a pitch cannot be just about product. It has to be about our product in relation to their buying decision criteria.

A pitch will position our solution in a way that introduces prospects to those elements that match their decision criteria and that they will find compelling enough to make a purchasing decision. But it must include not only solution data, but all of those aspects that the buyer needs to hear to know that the systems elements attached to the Identified Problem are managed.

Note:

- Pitch only after the buyer has decided what needs to happen for him/her to congruently bring in a new solution, including managing the necessary people/policy-based internal activity to achieve that;

- Only pitch once the buyer knows and shares;

- what information the decision team needs to help them decide;

- why they need it and what will happen if they are missing the data;

- how having the data will specifically rematch their end result.

Objections

There are no objections when you use Buying Facilitation® After all, objections are merely a defense against being pushed by sellers to consider changing when they aren't ready to change. Once they have bought in to change and bringing in a new solution, and when solutions are presented after the buying decisions have been made, there is no need for objections.

Members of the Buying Decision Team

The members of the Buying Decision Team must manage all of the people and policies and rules and elements that in any way touch the Identified Problem and need to buy in to a solution. They include:

- the managers who head up the areas that in any way touch the Identified Problem,

- representatives of those involved with the work-arounds or those working with familiar vendors who have provided the solutions until now;

- users who directly benefit from the new solution;

- people who work alongside solution providers; and

- historic relationships that may be changed.

Here are a couple of examples of members of a Buying Decision Team:

A web design solution would include the sales and marketing heads; programmers or tech folks responsible for any software that will work with, or be replaced by, the new solution; department heads who will have their offerings up on the site; bloggers or other professionals who will engage in social networking; numbers crunchers; psychologists or those who are responsible for creating Relationship Capital.

Another example would be:

A training solution, which would include inside folks who have done training until now; department heads of the groups who will be trained; people who will make sure that the new material will meld with the current material (maybe old vendors, or folks who wrote or used the existent material); the folks who will be trained.

DEFINITIONS

Buying Facilitation®: The Buying Facilitation® Method is a decision facilitation tool that helps buyers maneuver through their off-line, hidden, behind-the-scenes systems issues to enable them to bring together the appropriate elements that need to buy in for a product purchase.

System: A system is a conglomeration of conscious and unconscious, defined and assumed, elements that reside within a person, group, or entity (such as a school, family corporation, team) and that make the entity operate uniquely. Systems contain numerous idiosyncratic elements –all unique—that define the system, filter in and out who/what belongs in the system, and remain in the system throughout its life.

Identified Problem: A gap in the ability to be excellent—something missing that makes the system function inadequately, and demands work-arounds until a permanent fix is chosen and welcomed into the system.

Decision: A decision is a series of conscious and unconscious choices that result in change that maintains the integrity of the whole. In other words, decisions must be congruent with the rules and agreements of the underlying environment, and certain not to create chaos for the system.

Buying Decision Team: Those people in the buyer's organization that are in any way involved with managing the new solution, or in any way touch the Identified Problem and would experience some fallout if the Identified Problem were to change.

ABOUT THE AUTHOR

SHARON DREW MORGEN is the visionary behind Buying Facilitation®, the decision facilitation model that guides people through their behind-the-scenes decisions they must make to enable them to add a new solution and change with integrity. She is also the developer of HOBBES©, the search tool that gives site visitors the capability to get to that one page that will match their needs, and The eXpediter© the PDA decider that puts Buying Facilitation® into the user's hands, on demand.

Sharon Drew is a pioneer who has spoken about, written about, and taught the skills to help buyers buy. She coined the terms 'helping buyers buy,' 'decision facilitation,' and Buying Facilitation®.

Sharon Drew has been the founder and Managing Director of a European technology company, an international consultant and entrepreneur, a keynote speaker, trainer, management coach, and author of many books, including the acclaimed *New York Times* Business Bestseller *Selling with Integrity: Reinventing Sales Through Collaboration, Respect, and Serving* which is considered to be a sales classic and was voted one of the top nine sales books of the 20th century.

In an earlier life, Sharon Drew was a journalist, a social worker, a probation officer, a sales director, a stockbroker on Wall Street, and an insurance agent. She was also the Founder of The Dystonia Society, a non-profit organization that supports people with the muscle disorder Dystonia, from which her son George suffers.

Sharon Drew lives in Austin, TX. Her favorite joy is dancing.

INDEX